The Da Vinci Code in the Academy

The Da Vinci Code in the Academy

Edited by

Bradley Bowers

CAMBRIDGE SCHOLARS PUBLISHING

The Da Vinci Code in the Academy, edited by Bradley Bowers

This book first published 2007 by

Cambridge Scholars Publishing

15 Angerton Gardens, Newcastle, NE5 2JA, UK

British Library Cataloguing in Publication Data
A catalogue record for this book is available from the British Library

ISBN 1-84718-129-5; ISBN 13: 9781847181299

TABLE OF CONTENTS

INTRODUCTION

The question is obvious: Why *The Da Vinci Code*?

Why has one novel among many recent and similar novels, one fictional work among many speculative works over the last fifty years, one presentation of "facts" as "fiction" captured the imaginations and the interest of both the common reader and the critical academic?

The answer is both obvious and obscure, like *The Da Vinci Code*'s sources and secrets. To find an answer, or perhaps several answers, I have asked a number of scholars—religious, literary, cultural—to examine the cultural phenomenon which has become *The Da Vinci Code* controversy.

Specifically, these critics go beyond the continuing debate over the validity of sources and stories, of histories and alternative histories. They look at this text in terms of the controversy which it has caused, and why it has caused such controversy. It is easy to observe that *The Da Vinci Code* has been a powerful catalyst. The intriguing question for academics and other cultural observers: a catalyst in what mixture of forces, ideas, values? One book has functioned to trigger a cultural explosion, but what were the ingredients, waiting to react? What made *The Da Vinci Code,* if I may borrow a current cultural analogy, into *The Perfect Storm*?

One thing is clear: the answer always manifests itself at the intersection of fact and fiction. Every scholarly debate, in one way or another, returns to these fundamental questions: What is fact? What is fiction? This phenomenon has been our first date, culturally speaking, with postmodernism. This rising chorus of voices is the first popular awareness of the unraveling of authority proposed by the postmodern dilemma.

A Code To Live By

Regardless of what one thinks of Dan Brown's novel *The Da Vinci Code*, a couple of facts are indisputable. Individually, tens of millions of people worldwide have read the novel. Publicly, it has gotten a lot of attention. That's a bit of an understatement. This one contemporary novel has generated at least fifty other books which claim to explain, to debunk, to criticize, or to capitalize on the attention. Likewise, universities have created courses to do the same. Conferences have been held worldwide, including in Leonardo's hometown of Vinci, Italy, mostly to debate the factual errors, the historical inaccuracies, the flawed theories—contained in this fiction. Even the Vatican itself has joined the debate, one which will surely continue for years.

We, however, are not concerned only with alleged errors or inaccuracies, at least not those that may or may not be contained in this novel. We are concerned with the perhaps unprecedented reaction to a popular novel by otherwise sober academics and their institutions, by religious leaders and organizations more often concerned with people's souls rather than a book's sales, by the common readers who seem so impassioned by a retelling of the passion of the Christ which previously had become for so many passé.

The Da Vinci Code, like it or not, has entered the academy. And so we begin to look—not at the book's veracity—but at our collective reaction to what is now a debate beyond one book, but a debate about all of our stories.

Be they scholarly or popular, religious or radical, sacred or profane, these are the codes we live by.

Postmodernism Meets the Masses

At a conference, we were talking about *The Da Vinci Code* controversy, about why this novel has become more than a novel. That was the key, we agreed. It's not about Brown, the novel, or Leonardo da Vinci. It is the rekindling of *desire*, desire to reconnect with the divine in a world which has been robbed of divine secrets and stripped of divine codes, a world which continues to erase the wisdom of the ancients, and which denies that our stories can contain truth, even a glimpse of it.

It's the postmodern dilemma. Everything is a text. But . . . what do we need to survive? We need a text. We need a story. We need our stories. We have always had stories, and for most of human history, stories were true.

Stories were, and are, where we keep the truth, or at least something close to it. The novel's speculations about history and religion do not so much suggest lies as they suggest that truth, and true stories, still exist. Leonardo knew it, as did many, many writers, artists, and everyday folks throughout our existence on this planet. People throughout history have solved problems and dilemmas large and small, by recognizing the underlying divinity of human existence.

That is, until the twentieth century.

"Where is now thy God?" (Catholic Prayer Book, 1662)

The Da Vinci Code phenomenon is a reaction to a century-long process: access to the divine realm of human existence has been lost, severed by the rise of, first, modernism, and then, postmodernism, which have reduced all of our stories to texts, including our most sacred mythologies. Brown's novel has touched a nerve by suggesting that we could perhaps reconnect to our stories, that our mythologies once again could be true.

For most of our collective history, our stories revealed the real connection between human experience and that which is beyond human experience, that is, beyond rational human understanding. Through our participation in these stories, in our mythologies, we could experience, intuit, feel, and know something of what is beyond.

Now all of our stories—myth, legend, religion, history, opinion, news, novels, films--are only texts, devoid of the authority they once had.

Why?

A text is written by a human being. A text can be changed. A text does not reveal fundamental truth, divine truth, by providing a story that *can* be understood by a human being. A text is simply a manipulation of words.

Dan Brown's *The Da Vinci Code*, whose preface claims that all "descriptions of . . . documents and secret rituals in this novel are accurate," has achieved tremendous success and notoriety. Why? The novel has introduced millions of people to the postmodern paradox: if everything's a text these days, where do we find truth? Over the last century, we have accepted that all of the codes we live by are really just stories, just texts, and texts are not truths. Now, Brown's novel has confronted millions with that dilemma by suggesting that alternative texts may exist and may have as much, or even greater, authority than the standard versions.

The Contributors

Robert Davis examines the underlying issue of the sacred feminine, and his is a masterful description of the origins and resurgence of the goddess figure today in the discussion of this novel and in a number of other forums. He offers an intriguing explanation for *The Da Vinci Code*'s incredible popularity based on a re-manifestation of the sacred feminine, especially in American culture, fostered by the feminist and post-feminist re-visioning of religion and history over the last fifty years. Also, he offers a meticulous explication of why this popular novel forced its way into academic debates. His analysis, as many of the other analyses, touches on the rise of feminism, the weakening of the traditional church, the loss of textual authority in a globally connected world, and the continuing need for divine authority in a globally confused world. Ultimately, the nexus of the debate falls into the inevitable postmodern gap. Its most recent return, popularized by a novel, began almost a century ago. It blossomed as we approached the twenty-first century, only to explode in recent years, a phenomenon of a culture, he writes, "obscurely dissatisfied with its moral and spiritual inheritance."

Deanna Thompson takes a revealing look at the controversy, and she concludes that the debate itself is not actually centered on feminism, not specifically fueled by the idea of sacred feminine. The focus of the controversy is on sex, and she leads us on a field trip back in time to meet some early Christians.

Rachel Wagner looks carefully at the bases of the debates, and she reveals a set of Chinese boxes, each text revealing a previous text as its basis. Her analysis of the controversies goes beyond the written texts under discussion as sources. The texts being called into question by all sides are the texts of credentials, experience, study—our life texts which give authority to those who inhabit them—whether academic or clergy, professor or priest, scholar or saint. The reason for *The Da Vinci Code* debate is made clear: postmodernism is the new Gnosticism; relativism, the enemy of Christian faith.

Arlette Poland, likewise, takes us back to visit early Christianity. Poland's approach suggests that the solution lies not in the truth or fiction of the texts (whether ancient or modern) but in experience itself. She does, however, recognize the immense importance of texts in shaping our experience of the divine, especially the divine feminine.

Rosa Maria Stoops presents another unique perspective on the controversy. As both an academic and a Catholic, she explores the ironies of Brown's novel and its subsequent debaters, so ready to question the authority of traditional texts and teachings, while so eager to accept the authority of alternative texts and theories. She places the charge of systemic discrimination against women into the context of Catholic Church history, up to and including the positions taken by Pope John Paul II. Like many of the other critics here included, her analysis reveals that the popular polemic debates often oversimplify and misrepresent the issues at hand.

Harry Brown examines the novel as a new Grail quest, which it purports to be. While he agrees that the phenomenon of the novel's popularity has parallels with the tremendous popularity of the Grail legends of centuries past, he enumerates the differences among *The Da Vinci Code*'s version and the various manifestations of the divine feminine as part of the Grail quest stories. His conclusion points to a specific but elusive underlying reason for the book's twenty-first century impact.

Our last essayist points out that *The Da Vinci Code* is not the heretical treatise it has been made out to be. If we read carefully, we may actually come to the opposite conclusion.

Jennifer Brandt writes about the detective genre, and she reveals that the popular debate often misses the point. She argues that the novel is not a model for feminism, inside or outside of the Church. She suggests that this detective thriller is truly just that, conforming to almost every expectation and stereotype.

Her analysis challenges the premises of those who suggest that Brown's novel presents anything new, different, or contrary to the patriarchal standards for gendered behaviors.

The Awakening

This exploration of the reaction to a novel has paralleled an experience I have every spring. I have the pleasure of seeing a mind's awakening, expanding, comprehending, seeing in a way not yet imagined. It seems profound, and in some way it is, but it is also a quite normal process of intellectual growth. Let me explain.

Every spring for the last ten years, I have taught a first-year course which I created for the Honors program at my university. It replaces the standard Introduction to Literature course required of almost all students, because most students in the Honors program have already been introduced quite thoroughly to literature. Titled Twentieth Century Literature and Culture, it is designed not only to enhance their appreciation of literature but also to provide an introduction to literary theory and its linguistic underpinnings. The students are always from diverse disciplines and diverse cultures, which I have found provides the perfect cauldron for preparing this potion.

In short, these bright first-year students, most recently out of high school, are introduced first to the premises of Modernism, as distinguished from Romanticism, broadly defined. By spring break, we are moving into Postmodernism, and they are thoroughly uncomfortable with the breakdown of certainty and stability. However, by the time we reach the final weeks, they are not only comfortable with the postmodern dilemma, they also feel extremely empowered by this heretofore secret knowledge. They are further comforted by their understanding that this knowledge is reserved only for the initiate. Only those who have endured the process (in this case, Honors English) will know the code. The initiates have been given a power to understand how a text is created and maintained, but more importantly, how they themselves can alter, indeed create, new texts to serve their needs.

Why have scholars worldwide reacted with such vehemence to a detective novel?

The postmodern dilemma is not necessarily new to intellectual understanding. However, it has recently been magnified by our proliferation of texts and global communication. It has been said that the Internet makes every person on the planet an author and publisher, and with this change, the conditions that grant a text authority are being lost. An accepted text, an authoritative text, must have readers who accept that authority. And we are in the process of losing millions and millions of readers, who are being replaced with millions and millions of writers, all of whom have more or less equal authority.

It is the sacred or divine feminine, the goddess figure who plays the critical role in this retelling of history and religion. This feminine archetype of power and divinity is central to the study of religion, history, and literature. It is also one which today plays an iconic role in postmodern cultural studies, as well as psychology, sociology, folklore, and linguistics.

The novel has become a proxy debate for two of the most compelling scholarly and social issues of our time: the feminist/post-feminist challenge to patriarchal authority; and the textual construction of meaning and value. Combined, these represent the intersection of two of the most inflammatory academic and social conflicts of the late twentieth and early twenty-first centuries.

Divinity, femininity, and dominance, all mixed in with Leonardo da Vinci, a detective story, and a little romance. The answer becomes obvious.

CHAPTER ONE

THE WORKS OF THE FEMALE: MARY MAGDALENE AND THE RETURN OF THE GODDESS

ROBERT A. DAVIS, UNIVERSITY OF GLASGOW

> When Salome inquired when the things concerning which she asked should be known, the Lord said: When ye have trampled on the garment of shame, and when the two become one and the male with the female is neither male nor female...In the Gospel according to the Egyptians...they say that "the Savior himself said: I have come to destroy the works of the female."
> —Clement of Alexandria, *Stromata*, iii

> Jesus was the original feminist.
> —Lee Teabing to Sophie Neveu (Brown 334)

Robert Langdon's "three hundred page draft—tentatively titled *Symbols of the Lost Sacred Feminine*" (Brown 43), perhaps sounds an unlikely addition to the publications list of a contemporary Harvard art historian and "symbologist" (98). Were it to appear in print, however, it would doubtless find the kind of mass readership of which most Harvard academics (with some famous exceptions) only dream. The audience for this kind of popular scholarship is considerable, drawn largely from educated professional classes estranged from the established religious traditions of Western society—most conspicuously Christianity—but retaining powerful attachments to generically "spiritual" and transcendental longings in the pursuit of which their characteristically modern and conflicted forms of affluence and education perform an enabling role (Hanegraaff, *New Age*, 514-525). This is the core constituency of the so-called New Age generation, alienated from the material conditions of production and consumption that simultaneously support and provoke those unfulfilled desires which alternative forms of contemporary spirituality promise, with varying degrees of confidence, to fulfil (Mears and Ellison 289-94). The imagery of these movements of religious feeling in modern society draws promiscuously on a rich variety of sources, which textbooks such as Langdon's intended volume exist to marketise and catalogue, systematising vaguely held intuitions into bodies of belief which mimic the doctrines of the major faiths—even as they also explicitly reproach them—and helping resolve the New Age experience into something like an emergent religion (Heelas 110-135).

In some important respects, the rich and variegated communities of New Age adherents nonetheless represent an anomaly in the history of ideas and in the master-narrative of religion in Western society. They were not scheduled to happen. According to the well-worn arguments of the secularisation hypothesis, which has been such a powerful motor in Enlightenment thought since the middle of the eighteenth century, organized religion was supposed to be doomed by the irresistible two-hundred-year advance of reason, science and the unprecedented material prosperity brought about by technological civilization (Wallis and Bruce 8-31). The myth of modernization has for some time presented several options for explaining the eventual fate of religion in the post-confessional world, but neither a return of religion as a public force nor its continuing capacity to shape people according to its own ethos and instill into them an enduring *habitus* was supposed to be among them (Villa 540-552). To be sure, very few thinkers expected religion to disappear quickly or completely with the expansion and ascendancy of industrial society. Typified by the sociologist Thomas Luckmann, most assigned religion to a provisional space in the private sphere where it would simply wither as the conditions of its existence (put simply, scarcity, subsistence and superstition) were gradually ameliorated (114-146). Religious institutions, it was assumed, would undergo a parallel process of internal secularization, adapting increasingly to the requirements of modern social structures while maintaining their residual religious symbolism, which would steadily mutate into alternative and wholly material forms of cultural expression such as art and recreation. Some analysts, such as Robert Bellah, imagined that national ideologies or civil religions would functionally replace religious traditions, or expected socially constructive religious values (such as charity or solidarity) to permeate modern societies elsewhere in headlong retreat from traditional forms of religious observance (164-189). Few were prepared for the global resurgence of religions as public forces and as the powerful shapers of religious subjects they now seem set to become in many parts of the globalised world (Berger 1-19).

Adherents of the range of philosophies and spiritualities embraced by the flexible terminology of the New Age complicate the narrative of secularisation still further. Their general suspicion of established authority, hierarchy and doctrinal allegiance actually endorses in important senses the secularist model of enhanced individualism, dissenting enquiry and freedom of thought—signature attitudes of the Enlightenment response to traditional religious belief and authority (Bruce 75-90). At the same time, New Age dissatisfaction with what is frequently regarded as the incomplete or attenuated account of human purpose implied by the Enlightenment paradigm, and with many of the social, cultural and environmental effects of secularisation, stands in uneasy tension with the elevation of reason and progress that are such mobilising concepts in the modern project. To the affront of Enlightenment apologetics, New Age polemic frequently critiques precisely those principles that the emissaries of the radical, materialist Enlightenment once believed would eventually sweep aside the obscurantism, charismatic hierarchy and irrationalism associated with the benighted ages of faith (Israel, 218-30). A specific object of New Age ethical dissatisfaction, indeed, is that area of rational endeavour seen by many champions of the inductive method to be the touchstone of serious intellectual advance—science. That the chief beneficiaries of modernity should question the most obvious manifestation of their emancipation from the constraints of nature is seen by many of its critics as the ultimate delusion of the New Age (Kaminer 189-219), while admirers of the movement discern in its response to science both the pedigree and the defining ethic of a genuinely distinctive worldview (Sheldrake 149-164).

Misconceived or prescient, the constellation of New Age values and attitudes which now plays such a prominent role in the popular imagination in Western society has a distinct and in many respects impressive genealogy. Understanding something of the alignment of forces within this heritage of ideas sheds revealing light upon the appeal of *The Da Vinci Code* to a contemporary readership and helps elucidate the complex of heterodox religious and spiritual abstractions that have proved so compelling for a significant segment of that readership. The notion of the sacred feminine is, it would appear, the most resonant and sensational of these concepts, striking deep chords within the novel's fanbase and beyond, coalescing with religious themes and intuitions in the wider culture and gathering up into its orbit a cluster of hopes and anxieties associated with the current state of the world and our reaction to it. Dan Brown's account of the sacred feminine may be in vital respects confused and diminished, and there may well also be far-reaching objections to be raised about the salience of the concept *per se* as a viable religious perspective on the multiple ambiguities of twenty-first century life. Nevertheless, the origins of the sacred feminine run to the heart of the New Age critique of both traditional religious orthodoxy and Enlightenment rationality. Understanding their place in the legacy of Western spirituality offers unique insights into the character of religious thought in late industrial culture. That *The Da Vinci Code* has created the critical space in popular culture for such an intervention is certainly to be welcomed.

Orthodox opponents of the New Age frequently contend that little of its theological content is, in fact, new. In this regard, it may be poorly served by its nomenclature. Certainly, subversive and alternative belief systems in which the female principle, however constructed, figures prominently have been central to the imaginings of Counter-Enlightenment protests against the rise of reason and modernity for several centuries. They perhaps achieve their most recognisable expression in the cultural productions of Romanticism, where they appear as essentially poetic and imaginary valorisations of nature and the earth, in contradistinction to what many artists and thinkers of the Romantic period perceived prophetically as the growing menace of industrialisation, urbanisation and technology (Bate 24-44):

> Sacred goddess, Mother Earth
> Thou from whose immortal bosom
> Gods, and men, and beasts have birth
> Leaf and blade, and bud and blossom.
> —P.B. Shelley, "Song of Proserpine" (Shelley 612)

Influential critics of Romanticism, such as Isaiah Berlin, have highlighted the extent to which Romantic ideologues projected backwards the sources of their protest on to a re-imagined version of antiquity and the religious imagery of the classical past—when, in the cadences of John Keats, "holy were the haunted forest boughs,/Holy the air, the water and the fire" (Keats 341). This process was far more complex and less crude than Brown's oversimplified stand-off between Christian and pagan, but it nonetheless included—and in a vital sense initiated—a deep-seated interrogation of Christianity within elements of Romantic literature, driven principally by the perceived complicity of the Church with the injustices and depredations of early industrial society (Berlin 21-46). Despite its frustratingly garbled account of these movements of ideas, *The Da Vinci Code* nevertheless succeeds in isolating the fundamentally theological and symbolic nature of the contest, echoing recent Romantic theory in its restatement of the centrality of religious conflict to this aspect of the rhetoric of Romanticism (Balfour 71-90). The ambivalent figure of the "Eternal Feminine" in High Romantic writing—made famous by that most ambiguous of Romantics, Johann Wolfgang von Goethe—has its origins in a promulgation of alternative mythologies, a concentration of symbolism and iconography around a strategic resistance to both the supposed patriarchal power of monotheistic religion and the presumed reductionism of instrumental reason and its unforgiving institutional, economic and political expressions (Hoeveler 111-133). In the formulation and enrichment of ideas such as the Eternal Feminine, Romantic artists often found themselves propelled to the fringes of their own orthodox religious and philosophical inheritance, drawn by the forbidden allure of the suppressed and subterranean traditions reportedly marginalised by both Christianity and the growing philosophical rationalism of the academies (Abrams 169-197). This esoteric body of belief included fashionable if outlandish Hermetic doctrines from the centuries immediately before and after Christ, in which something approaching an all-encompassing female divinity had been represented to her devotees by the canopy of the stars in the night sky. Equally potent for Romantic aesthetics was the trope of the mystical androgyny, found in an array of similarly arcane traditions, including the occult wisdom of the alchemists and the cabbala, as well as the secret teachings of Orphism and Neoplatonism—and which fed the Romantic temperament in its challenge to established normative definitions of gender and sexuality (Roberts, "Ethereal Chemicals"). In *The Da Vinci Code*, Brown makes much of classical Gnosticism as a primary source for the maintenance through history of a cryptic and counter-Christian devotion to the sacred feminine. The acquaintance of Romantic writers with Gnosticism was, however, uncertain and fragmentary, largely restricted to their knowledge of the tantalising but sparse citations left by the Gnostics' dismissive patristic opponents. Smitten by the seditious allure of Gnosticism, intellectually accomplished and wide-ranging writers such as Novalis, Shelley, and Victor Hugo brooded over these elusive sources, frequently drawn to the recovery of ancient heresy because of its mysterious resonance with the theological and philosophical conflicts of their own time. Nevertheless, these efforts fell far short of the maintenance of a continuous tradition of alternative wisdom preserved intact from the ancient past and transmitted unbroken to later generations of adherents (Hanegraaff, "Romanticism," 237-269). Ronald Hutton has used the inchoate and haphazard character of the resultant Romantic construction of the Eternal Feminine to point up precisely the *absence* of any systematic articulation of feminised divinity in Romantic literature, despite the dazzling catalogue of visionary female figures who populate Romantic epic—including, in the English tradition, archetypal representations such as Shelley's Asia, Blake's Enitharmon or Keats' hallucinatory priestess of the Titans, Moneta. Instead, Hutton has highlighted another, related repository of ideas within which a fully-fledged concept of the Goddess assumed, in the course of the nineteenth century, a shape and substance of enormous import to contemporary New Age spirituality (32-43).

The anticlerical and sceptical vector in Enlightenment thought found one of its principle targets in the Bible, which was to become the focus of intense scrutiny in European intellectual circles in the period after the Peace of Westphalia of 1648. This process was furthered by the growth of imperialism and the encounters between the European powers and a diversity of ancient and exotic civilizations—many of them immeasurably older than Christianity—to which the expansion of trade and empire in the early modern period swiftly led. Engagement with the cultures of remote societies was often driven, of course, by the imperatives of Christian mission and by aggressive territorial incursion on the part of the European powers across the globe. In the academies and universities of Europe the results of the confrontation with alien societies gave rise to a feverish debate, often at the fringes of approved scholarship, and frequently involving a corresponding critical reflection on Europe's own "primitive" foundations as reflected in the status of the Hebrew Scriptures and the meaning of classical mythology. Growing fascination with the "otherness" of colonised or appropriated cultures stimulated in certain circles a "comparativist" reassessment of the founding documents of the European worldview (Zammito 221-255). Initially, late seventeenth century thinkers such as Athanasius Kircher, Alexander Ross and John Turner attempted to comprehend the mythologies of other ancient or unfamiliar cultures by emphasising the historical and doctrinal priority of the Old Testament and the derivative character of all other belief systems, including those of the Egyptians, Greeks and Hindus. At a later stage, more progressive minds such as Thomas Burnet and Noel Antoine Pluche, influenced by the preference for deism over revelation, urged a rationalistic interpretation of heathen religions, finding in primitive religious belief a perfectly comprehensible compound of superstition and ignorance of the laws of nature. In Scotland, the classicist Thomas Blackwell and in Italy, Giovanni Vico—one of the greatest minds of the age—pioneered by the middle of the eighteenth century the first serious departure from these generally patronising and "scientific" perspectives, arguing, instead, for an account of both ancient myth and savage belief which viewed each as coherent, if sometimes debased, representations of sublime truths: what Blackwell chose to term the "pagan philosophy" (Ackerman 147-155).

The distinct idiom of the response to myth typified by Blackwell and Vico had a pronounced leaning towards syncretism: grouping together into capacious thematic categories otherwise disparate elements of belief systems often separated by vast distances of time and space. This was an essentially imaginative undertaking, of enormous appeal to artists, writers and philosophers intent upon the affirmation of an organic past with which to resist the fissiparous forces of modern, industrial disintegration (Hungerford 62-91). It is out of this impulse that there emerges in the late eighteenth century the first shadowy image of a Great Goddess, unifying in her iconography the elemental qualities of female deities from across the imperial possessions and from within the mythological inheritance of the West itself. Synthesisers and encyclopedists such as Jacob Bryant, Charles Dupuis and George Stanley Faber sought to aggregate the characteristics of the principal female divinities of both the ancient world and the newly discovered religions of India and the Far East around certain grounding concepts such as seasonal change, astronomical observation or cosmic maternity (Feldman and Richardson 244-268). The influence of scriptural paradigms continued to be of incalculable importance in this process, and Faber, especially, derived his unitary image of a Mother

Goddess from what he claimed was a race memory of Noah's Ark, teeming with life. The argument also fed, however, on the extensive quantities of new material reaching scholars from the writings of imperial travellers, missionaries and explorers. In his remarkable 1808 compilation from his journals and commonplace books, entitled "Essays on the Sacred Isles in the West," the English soldier and amateur antiquarian, Francis Wilford, equated a number of classical and Indic goddesses with one another, at one point pausing to notice the recurrence of the idea of whiteness in their names or appellations (Wilford 165-188).

A growing band of classicists took to this perception of their discipline, perhaps because it offered an overarching explanatory framework within which the volatile body of classical myth could at last be organised and interpreted. This was, of course, a widespread Enlightenment aspiration. In 1849, the German philologist, Eduard Gerhard, proposed that behind all of the diverse goddesses of ancient Greece there stood a single Mother Goddess, venerated in prehistory before the rise of a Bronze Age warrior society had eclipsed her worship (Gerhard 101-105). Echoed in the work of a generation of Continental classicists, convinced that the cultures of Mesopotamia and Persia—into which European colonial expansion was now proceeding apace—were the ancestor civilizations of the Greeks, the concept of the Mother Goddess reverberated into other social and political debates taking place more widely in European thought. The writer most closely associated with the initial popularisation of the Great Goddess hypothesis, J. J. Bachofen, was a Swiss lawyer, who, in his 1861 book *Das Mutterrecht*, made the important advance from identification of an ancient universal Goddess to the proposition that the religious and cultic arrangements associated with her veneration reflected the fact that the earliest human societies had in fact been matriarchal. Bachhofen's remarkable claim was to be of tremendous import in the promotion of the concept of the sacred feminine. Ironically for both its defenders and opponents, his original formulation of the theory rested upon an assumption for the most part conveniently ignored by his modern admirers. This was the view that the shift from a matriarchal to a patriarchal society represented evolutionary progress for humanity, as the aggressive, inventive cultures of the ancient Near East shook off the stifling influence of woman-centred but essentially static institutions (Bachofen 220-43).

The vision of a primordial Goddess shimmering behind all of the belief systems of the ancient world would have remained the preserve of armchair academics and antiquarians had it not been for the hold it gained in the course of the nineteenth century over the fledgling disciplines of archaeology and anthropology. An initially sceptical community of amateur field archaeologists, following in the footsteps of imperial travellers and administrators, fell into the habit of interpreting ancient and prehistoric religions in terms of the comparative, tribal and totemic categories by which orientalist scholarship had begun to classify—and regulate—many of the subject peoples of empire (Said 73-92). Projecting these specifications on to the distant past became a natural propensity of classicists and folklorists across Europe seeking explanatory frameworks through which to make sense of the emerging archaeological and ethnographic record. By the beginning of the twentieth century writers such as the medievalist Edmund Chambers and the hugely influential classicist, Jane Harrison, began to write openly of a Great Earth Mother, progenitor of all of the gods and goddesses of ancient Europe, whose traces could be found variously in Greek myth, in early medieval rite and custom and in traditional folktale and romance. As Ronald Hutton has shown, the conversion to the Goddess hypothesis in the first decade of the twentieth century of Sir Arthur Evans, celebrated excavator of the Aegean Bronze Age warrior civilizations of Crete, proved decisive in establishing a consensus around which vast and disparate deposits of archaeological and anthropological material from across Europe were to be subsequently interpreted (37-40). In the years immediately preceding the First World War, intellectuals such as Harrison, Dechelette and even Sir James Frazer himself had helped establish an academic consensus that seemed able to translate almost any selection of material from premodern society—literary, historical or cultic—into evidence in favour of the Goddess hypothesis. The argument could assume various guises, and in its detail led not infrequently to incompatible conclusions. A common trend, however, was for writers of varying levels of scholarly rigour to seize upon a place or a period in European or Asian antiquity and suddenly marshal a whole raft of discordant data in support of the presence of the Goddess. John Arthur Goodchild brought the analysis home, as it were, when he boldly asserted in his strange book of 1898, *The Light of the West*, that a Great Mother Goddess had been the overarching divinity of all of the peoples of "Celtic" Britain, with her cult centre at no less prominent a site than Glastonbury. This argument was to have lasting significance for the revival of interest in the sacred feminine in the British Isles, particularly because Goodchild, a medic and self-proclaimed psychic, openly called in his study for the revival of devotion to the Goddess in order to heal the ills of the modern world (Goodchild 124-144).

Goodchild, of course, possesses many of the hallmarks of eccentricity that would make adherence to the Great Goddess hypothesis such an easy target for mainstream scholarship in subsequent decades. His position signals an important shift, however, in the speculative traditions of the sacred feminine because of its openly partisan and theological slant, determinedly advocating a return to Goddess worship and matriarchy. It is also arguable that Goodchild's work, despite its fringe status, exposes to view the theological—indeed evangelical—impulse residing at the heart of the Goddess hypothesis almost from its origins. As an intrinsically oppositional position, disputing the hegemony of both Abrahamic monotheism and Enlightenment rationalism, and deliberately promoting marginalised or ignored traditions of belief, advocacy of the Great Goddess exhibits many of the features of a *heresy*, contesting the dominance of a powerful orthodoxy and posing, as heresies always do, a radically divergent account of religious and philosophical truth. Perhaps the most notorious example of the attempt to rewrite religious history by openly presenting the cult of the Goddess as an underground heresy was Margaret Murray's book *The Witch Cult in Western Europe* of 1921. Murray's work was destined to become a seminal text in the revival of modern paganism, because of its insistence that the medieval witch craze was a disguised form of Goddess worship, maintained by a conservative rural population largely untouched by Christianity and systematically persecuted by a frightened and misogynistic Church (Murray 19-28). No amount of subsequent refutation of Murray's methodology and her conclusions has dislodged her books from the consciousness of modern paganism and its feminist fellow-travellers. The continuing appeal of her ideas highlights the extent to which support for the sacred feminine is prepared to defy orthodoxy whether it comes in theological or academic forms (Simpson 89-96).

Brown's fiction-making is therefore perversely correct in repeatedly describing the doctrine of the sacred feminine in the terminology of a heresy, feared and despised by an anxious religious and political establishment, even if the account he then offers of its historical origins is, like Murray's before him, almost entirely anachronistic:

> The Priory believes that Constantine and his male successors successfully converted the world from matriarchal paganism to patriarchal Christianity by waging a campaign of propaganda that demonized the sacred feminine, obliterating the goddess from modern religion forever….The days of the goddess were over. The pendulum had swung. Mother Earth had become a *man's* world, and the gods of destruction and war were taking their toll. The male ego had spent two millennia running unchecked by its female counterpart. The Priory of Sion believed that it was this obliteration of the sacred feminine in modern life that had caused what the Hopi Native Americans called *koyanisquatsi*—"life out of balance"—an unstable situation marked by testosterone-fueled wars, a plethora of misogynistic societies, and a growing disrespect for Mother Earth (172-174).

Like all heresies, the doctrine of the sacred feminine rests upon the disputation of key religious and mythological texts. As we have seen, from its outset, the theory of a primordial, Goddess-worshipping matriarchy required a comprehensive hermeneutical re-visioning of the immense body of historical and textual material out of which the dominant narrative of Western civilization had been constructed. In its specifically anthropological ancestry, the theory drew obvious sustenance from the strain in late Enlightenment thought that subjected the Bible in general, and the New Testament in particular, to dissenting sceptical enquiry. Finding the Goddess involved the sifting of manipulated source material supposedly fashioned in the interests of prevailing antifeminist orthodoxies, whether these lay in the scriptures or in the canonical versions of classical myth. The interrogation of the Biblical tradition by German Higher Criticism in the nineteenth century participated in a similar endeavour: restoring from their residual remains in the scriptural texts the plurality of stories, beliefs and practices homogenised by later orthodoxy into a closed and theologically coherent system from which all alternative narratives had been rigorously effaced (Smith 173-179; Barr 32-59). Once again, Brown's understanding of the argument here is oversimplified and sensationalised, but his intuitions guide him towards a basically valid perception of the doctrinal struggles reflected in the construction of both the Old and the New Testaments. As Teabing remarks:

> "The Bible is a product of *man,* my dear. Not of God. The Bible did not fall magically from the clouds. Man created it as a historical record of tumultuous times, and it has evolved through countless translations, additions, and revisions....
>
> Jesus Christ was a historical figure of staggering influence, perhaps the most enigmatic and inspirational leader the world has ever seen... His life was recorded by thousands of followers across the land...More than *eighty* gospels were considered for the New Testament, and yet only a relative few were chosen for inclusion—Matthew, Mark, Luke, and John among them." (312-313)

Central to Brown's argument, of course, is the insistence that consolidation of the canon of the New Testament involved two related forms of exclusion or redaction. The first is the familiar one of Goddess apologetics: that the development of the dogmatic coherence of the New Testament repeated and intensified the patriarchal Judaic elimination of the Goddess from all understanding and experience of the sacred. The second is much more unusual: that the developing story of the one of the key actors in the New Testament drama—Mary Magdalene—is profoundly interwoven with the same process by which the sacred feminine was erased from the historical memory of the Christian faith. Although Brown's attempt to unite these two themes is not without precedent, in its final form it represents one of the most conspicuous contributions of *The Da Vinci Code* to the contemporary renewal of interest in the Great Goddess. Brown's writing shows some passing acquaintance with a vibrant tradition of New Testament scholarship that has for over a century promoted Mary Magdalene as a character of central importance to the ministry of Jesus and to the Apostolic witness of the early Church; whose standing was later deliberately minimised by the misogyny and jealousy of a male priesthood in the first few Christian centuries (Brock 177-216). There is little or no suggestion in this literature, however, that Mary Magdalene represented unorthodox or pagan perceptions of women or of spirituality. Indeed, recognition of her status in Jesus' ministry is frequently used by theologians to highlight Jesus' inclusiveness and the innovative gender equality of the first Christians, in contrast to the sexual norms of surrounding paganism (de Boer 41-56). Brown's modification, here, is to link the revaluation of the role of Mary Magdalene in the events of the New Testament to the revaluation of the feminine principle in the overall apprehension of religious truth.

This departure involves establishing a genealogy for the image of Mary Magdalene that somehow parallels the fortunes of the cult of the Great Goddess in the context of the rise of a powerful and hostile Church. As is by now well known, Brown is furnished with a crucial link between the two strands of his conception by the evidence of the Gnostic Gospels, and the glimpses they contain of an alternative biography of Mary. This is further enhanced by the (entirely specious) bloodline theory, the centrepiece of which is the secret marriage of Mary to Jesus and the descent of a hidden royal lineage from them (Brown 329-336; Baigent *et al* 346-355, 419-421). Aspects of this dual hypothesis have their origins in early Biblical criticism and in the first serious efforts by German theologians to question the composition and historicity of the Gospels. The profile of Mary Magdalene drawn by the Tubingen school of New Testament studies was consistent with the broader aim of reconstructing the background to the life of Jesus by downplaying the miraculous elements of the Gospels and filling in their biographical and historical omissions through reference to extra-canonical sources and informed conjecture. In this setting, supposition as to the nature of the companionship of Mary and Jesus could run free, leading a number of prominent scholars to surmise that intimacy may indeed have existed between them. Nineteenth century speculation stopped short, however, of the direct suggestion that the two were married, preferring to emphasise, instead, the dependence of the excitable and histrionic woman demoniac on the male charismatic leader in whose quiet service she found peace of mind (Haskins 328-331). The various components of Brown's underlying vision of the sacred feminine combine in an internally coherent synthesis of Goddess, Magdalene and New Age feminine principle only through a feat of the imagination, which can supply missing connections and elaborate a pattern of associations across highly differentiated material. It is therefore not surprising to discover that the most significant forerunners of Brown's portrait of Mary Magdalene and the Goddess can be found in two key areas—twentieth century historical fiction and the treasury of primary texts of early Christian Gnosticism unearthed by the archaeological findings at Nag Hammadi. Upon its discovery in 1945, this astonishing Fourth Century library revealed in something approaching a complete form the traditions of heretical Gnostic belief that had been known to the Romantics and their followers only in fragments. There is, of course, a relationship between these two sets of materials exploited by Brown, but it is a complex one. Some of the important novels in which a genuine anticipation of Brown's preoccupations may be detected were written long before, or in complete ignorance of, the Nag Hammadi documents. The Nag Hammadi texts themselves reflect a huge range of theological positions, of which classical Gnosticism is only one strain, and within which the role of a divine female principle is a sub-theme of uncertain provenance and doubtful meaning (Williams 54-76).

Nevertheless, it is certainly true that the Nag Hammadi cache, supplemented by other ancient Gnostic texts reappraised in the light of its discovery, provides the basis of an affinity between the figure of Mary Magdalene and a wider vision of the sacred feminine with which she is directly implicated in certain strains of Gnostic thought. Brown's version of this association is understandably novelistic, stressing the recognition of Mary as, first, Jesus' wife and lover and, secondly, as a mystical channel of the divine wisdom, the *Pistis Sophia*. The first of these propositions is, as we have demonstrated, a fringe and intermittent conjecture of a still broadly orthodox interpretation of the New Testament. The second, however, is a profound deviation from orthodoxy predicated upon a startlingly unconventional perception of the nature of the divine, wildly at odds with accepted Judeo-Christian dogma (King 83-93). Several Gnostic texts do indeed offer this portrait of Mary Magdalene as a favoured and ecstatic visionary, accorded privileged access to the secret teachings of Jesus, the uniqueness and prestige of which incurs the fear and resentment of the apostles (Haskins 37-43). A recurring motif of this writing is the erotically-charged metaphor of sacred marriage, though the status of the motif is hotly disputed in the context of the general Gnostic disapprobation of the body and sexuality (Calvert-Koyzis, "Re-sexing the Magdalene"). Similarly, the relative lateness of the Gnostic texts, when compared with, particularly, the synoptic Gospels, casts doubt on the perception of them as genuine, rival accounts of power and gender relations in the Early Church. They may, in fact, require to be read in the context of the prolific allegorical mythmaking of the later Gnostic temperament and its insistence on the priority of secret knowledge over witness and faith (Schaberg 297-318). Their indiscriminate sampling of the traditions of wisdom literature from Neoplatonism and Hermeticism is consistent with the decadent syncretism of the mystery religions that held such fascination for the pagan Alexandrian intellectual elites of the second and third centuries and whose imprint is stamped all over Gnostic theology.

Syncretism has been, as we have shown, a crucial process in the formation and defence of the sacred feminine from the Romantics onwards. *The Da Vinci Code* is a relentlessly syncretic venture, evidenced most clearly in the endless pseudo-scholarly digressions which fill out the narrative. Syncretism, it might be argued, is propensity of the myth-making mind, closely allied to conspiracy and paranoia. Umberto Eco's novel, *Foucault's Pendulum* famously ironises it as a method of historical enquiry: "I began to let myself be lulled by feelings of resemblance: the notion that everything might be mysteriously related to everything else" (139); "There are always connections; you have only to want to find them" (190); "The problem is to find occult links between, for example, the cabala, and the spark plugs of a car" (314). "So wanting connections, we found connections–always, everywhere and between everything. The world exploded into a whirling network of kinships, where everything pointed to everything else, everything explained everything else" (384). Several of the works of fiction that prefigure *The Da Vinci Code* repeat the same procedure, and it is through the power of their syncretic imaginings that they have made a decisive contribution to the dissemination of the sacred feminine as an appealing religious concept for the modern age.

Probably the most revealing and accomplished of these works is Robert Graves' 1946 novel *King Jesus*. Graves' chief contribution to the return of the Goddess to twentieth century religious awareness—and still widely underestimated in most studies of the phenomenon—is his 1948 work of poetic anthropology, in the tradition of Frazer and Harrison, *The White Goddess*. *The White Goddess* is a work of painstaking, even obsessive, erudition, reconstructing the presence of the Goddess behind patriarchal religious dogma––classical, Jewish and Christian—and providing her with a devotional poetic and cultic history. It is also, however, a manifesto, urging the revival of her veneration as an antidote to the bankruptcy of modern theism and the menace of scientific rationalism, which Graves sees as the secular heir to the patriarchal values of the recent religious past (Graves, *White Goddess* 465-479). The impact of Graves' ideas on the student and countercultural politics of the 1960s has never been properly appraised, but his combination of poetic devotion to the Muse and detailed defence of a matriarchal understanding of ancient religion and society carried his ideas to a readership largely untouched by abstruse academic debates (Psilopoulos 159-175). As a gifted novelist, Graves was also able to harness important aspects of his prose fiction of the 1940s to the same project: vindicating the experience of the Goddess and the worship of the sacred feminine and situating them in the imaginative portrayal of archaic cultures in which otherwise inaccessible scholarly claims might be sympathetically rendered and explored. *King Jesus* lies at the heart of this creative endeavour. Exhibiting a deep and knowledgeable indebtedness to the anthropological methods of the Cambridge School and the hermeneutics of the Higher Criticism, the novel recaptures the magical, conflicted character of first century Palestine in which the personality of Jesus is formed. In Graves' realization, this is a place of feverishly competing belief-systems, ethnic rivalries, brutal political intrigue, messianic expectations and endemic superstition. While undeniably dominant, the austere Jewish worship of "Jehovah," centred on the Jerusalem Temple, exists alongside residual and emergent religious practices that call into question its temporal authority and cultic credentials. The fictional universe of *King Jesus* pays homage to an alternative, healing, ceremonial conception of religious sentiment in which hidden, occult interpretations of seemingly unassailable orthodoxies represent not simply heresy, but a return to a kind of feminised and unifying religious innocence intimate with the mysteries of life, love, death and rebirth. Jesus is secretly and deliberately brought into the world by his royal parents to announce and inaugurate this cleansed and balanced perception of divinity. It is a perception epitomised by the sacred marriage of king and priestess, and which, it is intended, will culminate in the anticipated establishment of a purified socio-religious order under the sovereignty of the "the Great Triple Moon-goddess who is generally reputed to have mothered the Mediterranean races…" (Graves, *King Jesus* 8). The novel attains its unique level of human and theological interest, however, when it returns to the inner dynamic of the New Testament itself, presenting in its central character a figure whose appeal lies in his unexpected resistance to the onward drive and closure of the pagan matriarchal impulse, including his role in the sacred marriage. Graves' Jesus is a personality of commanding presence in the novel by virtue of his unflagging individualism—an extraordinarily intensified self-consciousness that refuses the immobilising surrender and loss of self implied in a preordained mythological destiny and opts instead to assert free choice and spiritual agency.

As a sacred King, the last legitimate ruler of an immensely ancient dynasty, his avowed intention was to fulfil all the ancient prophecies that concerned himself and bring the history of his House to a real and unexceptionable conclusion. He intended by an immense exercise of power and trust in God the Father to annul the boastful tradition of royal pomp…and at the same time to break the lamentable cycle of birth, procreation, death and rebirth in which he and his subjects had become involved since Adam's day. Merely to resign his claim was not enough. His resolute hope was to defeat Death itself by enduring with his people the so-called Pangs of the Messiah, the cataclysmic events which were the expected prelude to the coming of the Kingdom of God (239).

Jesus attains his spiritual autonomy in two ways: first, through the achievement of self-mastery in which all personal vices and appetites are subdued; secondly—and much more demandingly—through direct confrontation with the representatives of the pagan Goddess and what Jesus regards as her pernicious rites. The second of these tasks forms one of the major themes of the novel and is expressed in a series of dramatic encounters between Jesus and the remnant of the Goddess' followers. The most momentous of these is the contest with Mary the Hairdresser (Mary Magdalene). Mary is depicted in the novel as a seemingly outcast priestess of forbidden rites and holy icons, which she preserves as reminders to Israel of its repressed matriarchal, Goddess-centred past. The ritual confrontation between Jesus and Mary at the Terebinth Fair is a turning point in the novel. Graves goes to considerable lengths in the struggle to emphasise that Jesus is not simply ignorant of the Goddess, like so many of his naïve contemporaries. He in fact possesses an intimate understanding of her cult. He remains, nonetheless, her sworn adversary, "come to destroy the works of the Female" (191) and intent, quite literally, on writing her out of the sacred narratives of Israel by wresting from Mary the authority to interpret the ancient icons in her charge.

> A great contest ensued between Mary and Jesus over the interpretation of the pictures, and neither was ever at a loss for the word of contradiction.
>
> Mary said: "See where my Mistress, the First Eve, is seated on her birth stool under the palm tree. The people are awaiting a great event, for the pangs are upon her."
>
> Swiftly Jesus answered her: "No, witch that is not the First Eve: that is Deborah judging the Israelites under the palm-tree of Deborah. For so it is written." (213)

Jesus, once again by consummate force of will, finally breaks the resolve of Mary and wins the contest at the Terebinth Fair, proclaiming his intent to take spiritual authority forever away from the regressive claims of mother-right in the name of the fierce but benevolent Father God of the Jewish people. In one of the many ironies of *King Jesus*, it transpires that Jesus' boldest gestures of defiance in fact unintentionally lock him still more securely into his inescapable destiny as sacred king and sacrificial victim. Mary Magdalene and the Goddess therefore enjoy a kind of victory over Jesus as he is condemned to death on the Cross in the same fashion as the countless other consorts who have preceded him. Graves' Mary, though not the bride to whom Jesus is betrothed, combines in her role individual will and determination with hieratic access to the hidden religious truths of the divine feminine. In this fusion, she draws heavily on the Mary of Gnostic and other heresy while fully anticipating her pivotal function in the esoteric history that forms the backdrop to *The Da Vinci Code*.

What this connection underlines is a point made throughout this essay: that the return of the Goddess is fundamentally a cultural phenomenon of modern society, fulfilling a need and radiating through the intellectual and spiritual life of a culture obscurely dissatisfied with its moral and spiritual inheritance. It is a movement of feeling that seeks out, and makes use of, a range of resources routinely branded as heterodox, proscribed or anathema; seizing imaginatively upon peripheral or rejected beliefs wherever they are to be found and taking them up into a fully-developed protest against both religious and secular orthodoxies and the diminished accounts of human nature they continue to pedal. In this respect, the question of validity is a less relevant issue than the expressive potential of the concept itself—its enabling function within a broader economy of alternative spiritual realities. In the period between the publication of the novels *King Jesus* in 1946 and *The Da Vinci Code* in 2003, interest in the sacred feminine has burgeoned in both scholarly and popular circles all across the developed world. It seems fair to observe from the outset that almost every academic effort to reconstruct a coherent and convincing anthropology of the primordial Goddess and the supposed matriarchal civilization over which she once presided has failed to satisfy the criteria of historical verification (Eller 56-81; 93-116). The accumulation of circumstantial archaeological and folkloristic evidence presented by respected field researchers such as the archaeologist Marija Gimbutas has been seriously challenged by a community of sceptical anthropologists doubtful of the inclination in Goddess scholarship to favour survivalist models of culture and uncritical reconstructions of the attitudes and worldviews of the distant past based on the most problematic of data (Wood 19-23). The spirituality of modern feminism has been a crucial driver in this process, eschewing the Marxist, antireligious preferences of first wave feminism, but determined to articulate a vision of the transcendent free from the patriarchal assumptions of the monotheistic creeds and their damaging misogyny. Almost inevitably, this inflection of the Goddess hypothesis has, as a consequence, been drawn into the orbit of contemporary neopaganism and the synthesising philosophies of movements such as Wicca, with their omnivorous tendency to assimilate widely diverse religious and quasi-religious experiences into a single overarching narrative of feminine religious ontology, from palaeolithic ritual, through Mesopotamian myth, to mediaeval witchcraft (Gadon 233-257). There is, of course, no *prima facie* reason why the association of Goddess scholarship with openly religious organisations should invalidate its claims. The study of the Bible remains strongly rooted in the practice of Christian theology. However, rebuttal of the arguments in support of the existence of a primordial Goddess cult is made more difficult when it gets confused with repudiation of the sacred feminine itself, for the latter implies a delegitimation of perceptions that have assumed genuine meaning in the lives of many contemporary women. In a sense, the withdrawal of the concept behind the confines of popular fiction shelters it from this criticism, by exempting it from the tests of conventional scholarship—tests which many of its advocates believe to be fundamentally compromised by their inbuilt rationalist (and masculinist) epistemology.

Paradoxically, this point of apparent impasse may be the juncture at which some sort of evaluation of the significance of the so-called return of the goddess becomes possible without being merely adversarial. Defence of the sacred feminine, as its locus in imaginative writing suggests, is essentially a symbolic undertaking. It is certainly no coincidence that *The Da Vinci Code* is a text obsessed with symbolism and devoted in large measure to the interpretation of a colossal array of signs, symbols and cryptograms in which are encoded a tremendous religious secret. The act of interpretation involves the discernment of hidden meanings, but it may equally be seen as the *imposition* of sense and meaning upon otherwise intractable or unmediated material. At the heart of Langdon and Teabing's quest is a woman's name, a name that is also the signifier of the divine female principle, *Sophia*. Sophie Neveu, like Mary Magdalene, is cast in the novel as an individuated woman, but also as a conduit to the religious mystery that forms the centrepiece of Brown's argument. Interpreting the disputed symbolism of the Goddess is, in the end, an identity-conferring action and this may be its chief purpose all along: once again to invest female cultural identity with a spiritual purpose and to resist the story of patriarchal hegemony and suppression by retelling one of enduring female dignity and power, the wisdom and integrity of which may yet have bounty to communicate to the modern world. If this analysis is correct, the truth conditions of the sacred feminine shift perceptibly, away from historicism and back towards myth, in exactly the direction Simon Pembroke argued some thirty years ago the Goddess hypothesis is always destined to move. When the ancients spoke of matriarchal societies from their own remote past or in distant foreign lands, Pembroke suggests, they employed the concept normatively, as they did with the fearful notion of societies ruled by slaves, to justify—construct, even—their own forms of social organisation and cultural attachment. "Gynaeocracy," Pembroke states, "is women getting out of hand" (30). The triple claim of primordial Goddess, primitive matriarchy and pervasive sense of the sacred feminine simply reverses this strategy, by inducing a contemporary culture confronted on all sides by crises of its own making to question the complicity of its underpinning spiritual allegiances in the causes of these crises and to contemplate, perhaps at the moment of greatest danger, other more optimistic ways of configuring both the human and the divine.

Works Cited

Abrams, M. H. *Natural Supernaturalism: Tradition and Revolution in Romantic Literature*. New York: Norton, 1971.

Ackerman, Robert. "Writing About Writing About Myth." *Journal of the History of Ideas* 30 (1973), 147-155.
Bachofen, Johan J. Trans. R. Michaelson. *Myth, Religion and Mother Right.* New Jersey: Bollingen, 1967.
Baigent, Michael, Leigh, Richard and Lincoln, Henry. *The Holy Blood and the Holy Grail.* 2nd Edition. London: Random House, 1996.
Balfour, Ian. *The Rhetoric of Romantic Prophecy.* Stanford: Stanford University Press, 2002.
Barr, James. *History and Ideology in the Old Testament: Biblical Studies at the End of a Millennium.* Oxford: OUP, 2000.
Bate, Jonathan. *The Song of the Earth.* Basingstoke: Picador, 2000.
Bellah, Robert N. *The Broken Covenant: American Civil Religion in Time of Trial.* Chicago: University of Chicago Press. 2nd edition, 1992.
Berger, Peter L. "The Desecularization of the World: A Global Overview." The *Desecularization of the World: Resurgent Religion and World Politics.* Ed. Peter Berger et al. Grand Rapids, MI: Eerdmans, 1999. 1-19.
Berlin, Isaiah. *The Roots of Romanticism.* Ed. Henry Hardy. London: Chatto and Windus, 1999.
Brock, Ann Graham. *Mary Magdalene, The First Apostle: the struggle for authority.* Cambridge, Mass: Harvard University Press, 2003.
Brown, Dan. *The Da Vinci Code.* London: Corgi, 2004.
Bruce, Steve. *God is Dead: Secularization in the West.* Oxford: OUP, 2002.
Calvert-Koyzis, Nancy. "Re-sexualizing the Magdalene: Dan Brown's Misuse of Early Christian Documents in *The Da Vinci Code.*" *Journal of Religion and Popular Culture* 12 (Spring 2006) [150606]. http://www.usask.ca/relst/jrpc/art12-resex.html.
de Boer, Esther. Trans. John Bowker. *Mary Magdalene: Beyond the Myth.* London: SCM Press, 1997.
Eco, Umberto. *Foucault's Pendulum.* London: Picador, 1988.
Eller, Cynthia. *The Myth of Matriarchal Prehistory.* Boston: Beacon Press, 2000.
Feldman, Burton and Richardson, Robert D. *The Rise of Modern Mythology, 1680-1860.* Bloomington, Ind.: Indiana University Press, 1972.
Gadon, Elinor. *The Once and Future Goddess: A Symbol for Our Time.* San Francisco, CA: Harper and Row, 1989.
Gerhard, Eduard. *Uber Metroen und Gotter-Mutter.* Berlin, 1849.
Goodchild, John Arthur. *The Light of the West.* London: Kegan Paul, 1898.
Graves, Robert. *The White Goddess.* Ed. Grevel Lindop. Manchester: Carcanet, 1997.
—. *King Jesus and My Head! My Head!* Ed. Robert A. Davis. Manchester: Carcanet, 2006.

Haskins, Susan. *Mary Magdalen: The Essential History*. 2nd Edition. London: Pimlico, 2003.

Hanegraaff, Wouter J. *New Age, Religion and Western Culture: Esotericism in the Mirror of Secular Thought*. Leiden: Brill, 1996.

—. "Romanticism and the Esoteric Connection." *Gnosis and Hermeticism: From Antiquity to Present Times*. Ed. Roelf van den Broek and Wouter J. Hanegraaff. New York: SUNY Press. 1997: 237-269.

Heelas, Paul. *The New Age Movement: The Celebration of the Self and the Sacralization of Modernity*. Oxford: Blackwell, 1996.

Hoeveler, Diane. *Romantic Androgyny: The Women Within*. Pennsylvania: Penn State University Press, 1999.

Hungerford, Edward Buell. *Shores of Darkness*. New York: Columbia UP, 1941.

Hutton, Ronald. *The Triumph of the Moon: A History of Modern Pagan Witchcraft*. Oxford: OUP, 1999.

Israel, Jonathan. *Radical Enlightenment: Philosophy and the Making of Modernity, 1650-1750*. Oxford: OUP, 2001.

Kaminer, Wendy. *Sleeping with Extra-Terrestrials: The Rise of Irrationalism and Perils of Piety*. New York: Pantheon, 1999.

Keats, John. *The Complete Poems*. Ed. John Barnard. London: Penguin, 1988.

King, Karen L. *The Gospel of Mary of Magdala: Jesus and the First Woman Apostle*. Santa Rosa, CA: Polebridge Press, 2003.

Luckmann, Thomas. *The Invisible Religion: The Problem of Religion in Modern Society*. London: MacMillan, 1967.

Mears, Daniel P. and Ellison, Christopher G. "Who Buys New Age Materials? Exploring Sociodemographic, Religious, Network, and Contextual Correlates of New Age Consumption." *Sociology of Religion* 61.3 (Fall 2000): 289-313.

Murray, Margaret. *The Witch Cult in Western Europe*. London: OUP, 1921.

Pembroke, Simon. "Women in Charge: The Function of Alternatives in Early Greek Tradition and the Ancient Idea of Matriarchy." *Journal of the Warburg and Courtauld Institutes*. 30 (1967): 1-35.

Psilopoulos, Dionysious. "Robert Graves, the Esoteric Tradition, and the New Religion." *New Perspectives on Robert Graves*. Ed. Patrick J. Quinn. London: Associated University Presses, 1999.

Roberts, Maureen B. "'Ethereal Chemicals': Alchemy and the Romantic Imagination." *Romanticism On the Net*, 5. (February 1997) [150606]. http://users.ox.ac.uk/~scat0385/alchemy.html.

Said, Edward. *Orientalism*. Harmondsworth, Penguin, 1985.

Schaberg, Jane. *Resurrection Of Mary Magdalene: Legends, Apocrypha, And The Christian Testament*. London: Continuum, 2004.

Sheldrake, Rupert. *The Rebirth of Nature: The Greening of Science and God.* Paris, Maine: Park Street Press, 1994.

Shelley, Percy Bysshe. *Poetical Works*. Ed. Thomas Hutchinson and G. M. Matthews. London: OUP, 1970.

Simpson, Jacqueline, "Margaret Murray: Who Believed Her and Why?" *Folklore* 105 (1994): 89-96.

Smith, Mark, S. *The Origins of Biblical Monotheism: Israel's Polytheistic Background and the Ugaritic Texts*. Oxford: OUP, 2001.

Villa, D. "Max Weber: Integrity, Disenchantment, and the Illusions of Politics." *Constellations* 6.4 (December 1999): 540-560.

Wallis, Roy and Bruce, Steve. "Secularization: The Orthodox Model." *Religion and Modernization: Sociologists and Historians Debate the Secularization Thesis*. Ed. Steve Bruce. Oxford: The Clarendon Press, 1992. 8-31.

Wilford, Francis. "Essays on the Sacred Isles in the West." *Asiatick Researches* 11, 1810.

Williams, Michael. *Rethinking "Gnosticism": An Argument for Dismantling a Dubious Category*. Princeton, NJ: Princeton University Press, 1999.

Wood, Juliette. "The Concept of the Goddess." *The Concept of the Goddess*. Ed. Sandra Billington and Miranda Green. London, Routledge, 1996. 8-26.

Zamitto, J. H. *Kant, Herder, and the Birth of Anthropology*. Chicago: University of Chicago Press, 2001.

CHAPTER TWO

JESUS LOVED HER MORE THAN THE REST: MARY MAGDALENE, THE SACRED FEMININE, AND WHAT'S REALLY BEEN COVERED UP

DEANNA THOMPSON, HAMLINE UNIVERSITY

> "According to these unaltered gospels, it was not *Peter* to whom Christ gave directions with which to establish the Christian Church. It was *Mary Magdalene*."
>
> Sophie looked at him. "You're saying the Christian Church was to be carried on by a *woman*?"
>
> "That was the plan. Jesus was the original feminist. He intended for the future of His Church to be in the hands of Mary Magdalene."
>
> —D. Brown 248

Out of the pages of Dan Brown's conspiracy thriller Mary Magdalene rises to a level of stardom in church and popular culture never witnessed before. An ABC television special and countless news articles delving into her image as Jesus' beloved companion, even nation-wide church forums committed to deciphering *The Da Vinci Code* for contemporary believers all wrestle with Brown's claim that the powers-that-be in Christianity have staged a massive cover-up about the true identity of Mary, and the power of the "sacred feminine" in the original version of Christianity.

But is all this hoopla about the sacred feminine and Mary's "true" identity good for feminist Christianity? Is claiming that Jesus was the "original feminist" and married to Mary Magdalene unveiling to the world a vision feminists should embrace?

In my conversations with many *Da Vinci Code* fans, particularly women, I hear great enthusiasm for the elevation of women and the feminine in connection with the Christian tradition that is overburdened by patriarchy and masculine symbols. From the smart and ultra-competent Sophie Neveu to the resurrecting of the power of Mary Magdalene that has allegedly been covered up, readers of Brown's thriller are seemingly given an alternative version of female strength, both past and present. Women who read this feel empowered. Especially my Catholic students report to me that *The Da Vinci Code* asks and answers many pressing questions about the sexism of the Church that they have secretly entertained themselves.

But feminist scholars of religion must press the question: is the portrayal of the feminine in *The Da Vinci Code* actually an empowering one? There are several possible reasons to answer in the negative. We can, for example, offer an analysis of Miss Neveu, who for all her smarts is still described in physical terms in a way the male characters are not, and in the end is placed predictably in a "boy saves girl" drama. Or we can side with a Catholic priest I heard at one of these popular church forums: when discussing Brown's attention to ancient fertility rites, the priest commented: "Brown's not interested in fertility, he's interested in sex."

The priest, I believe, is on the right track. A major reason feminist scholars should not give Brown and the avalanche of attention to Mary Magdalene a ringing endorsement has primarily to do with the treatment of sexuality in Brown's conspiracy, particularly as it relates to the depiction of femininity in the novel. I stand with the many scholars who bemoan Brown's bad representation of history (such as his claim that the Hieros Gamos sex ritual is somehow related to Mary Magdalene), his exploitation of certain historical uncertainties (such as the marital status of Jesus and Mary Magdalene), and his conflation of sexual tension with an uncovering of the power of the sacred feminine. The list could go on. Brown deserves serious critique for over-simplification (to claim, for instance, that the status of sexual intercourse went from good to bad within Christianity) that betrays the complexities and messiness of religious historical developments and the gendered roles therein. We could, perhaps, attempt a counter-argument to these critiques, insisting that it's only a novel, after all; it's all just fiction anyway. But when Brown begins the novel with a page entitled "Fact," which states that most descriptions in the novel are "real," "factual," or "accurate," I think he deserves a "D-" for his attempt at credibility in the areas of art, history, and religion.

That said, I must confess that despite its problems, I loved reading *The Da Vinci Code.* I couldn't put it down. The years this book sits at the top of the New York Times Bestseller list—accompanied now by a big-screen version of itself—suggest that not only do millions of us still love a conspiracy, but millions of us also seem quite taken with the idea that Christians have been duped into accepting a male-dominated version of religion. In addition, I, likely along with many of you, have marveled at the way in which Brown's novel has ushered early church history and questions about the role of women within Christianity into popular and ecclesial conversations. Besides finding it an enjoyable read, my enthusiasm for *The Da Vinci Code* comes from its striking ability to get people into books, forums, even courses about Jesus, Mary Magdalene, non-canonical texts, and ancient Christianity in general. Nevertheless, I want to challenge the claims that Brown advances a feminist agenda in his novel. Closer inspection of Brown's version of feminine power in Mary Magdalene, Sophie Neveu, and the sacred feminine reveals both a stereotypical view of femininity and a surprising lack of power. Then a brief tour through the messy world of ancient Christianity will demonstrate that female power did indeed exist within the ancient church, but quite differently from the way imagined by Dan Brown.

Brown's Leading Lady: Mary Magdalene and Feminine Power

Dan Brown deserves credit for calling the public's attention to the lamentable misrepresentation of Mary Magdalene by the church and society for over a millennium. Brown is correct: Mary Magdalene of the gospels—both canonical and non-canonical—is not depicted as a prostitute. In the gospels of Mark (16.9) and Luke (8.2), Mary is described as one who suffers from demon possession, having seven demons cast out of her by Jesus. Most would agree with Brown that Pope Gregory's sixth century sermon relegated this Mary to prostitute status when he equated her with the unidentified "sinful" woman in Luke 7.37-50. Some scholars call Pope Gregory's sermon evidence of a conspiracy that aims to separate the pure, virginal mother-of-Jesus Mary from the apostate, sinner-turned-repentant Mary Magdalene (King qtd. in Roberts). Others argue Pope Gregory had no malicious intent; instead, he found this repentant Mary worthy of emulation (Olson and Miesel 78-86). Regardless of the Pope's motive, we bemoan the malignant effects this conflation of biblical stories has had on the reputation of Mary Magdalene. And we applaud Dan Brown for calling widespread attention to the necessary rehabilitation of Mary Magdalene's status.

But Brown does not stop there. Not only was Mary not a prostitute; in fact, Brown relies upon several non-canonical gospels to assert that Mary and Jesus were joined in marriage. Brown cites a passage from the Gospel of Philip where the disciples ask Jesus, "Why do you love her more than all of us?" (246); the text continues with a reference to Jesus kissing Mary.[1] While it may be tempting to infer that such references indicate a sexual relationship, most scholars dispute

[1] The particular passage quoted by Brown is full of gaps in the existing version of the Gospel of Philip. It reads: "And the companion of the [small gap in the manuscript] Mary Magdalene [small gap] her more than [small gap] the disciples [small gap] kiss her [small gap] on the [gap]" (Bart Ehrman, *Lost Christianities* 122).

Brown's literalistic interpretation of this highly mystical text.[2] Further, many scholars agree that marriage between Jesus and Mary was unlikely (P. Brown 33-64).

But let's stay with Brown's depiction of Jesus' and Mary's relationship for a moment. What does marriage do for this female follower of Jesus? On one level, Mary's status appears to be greatly exalted. Not only is she closer to Jesus than any other human being, but her feminine power carries on through birthing their child and according to Brown, through carrying on Jesus' church before her power is usurped by men. Upon closer examination, however, to claim marriage as Mary's link to Jesus, scholar Bernadette Brooten notes, discredits her status as a prostitute but still leaves sexuality intact as the linchpin of her identity (qtd. on "Speaking of Faith"). Mary's prominent roles in the crucifixion and resurrection narratives within the biblical text—not to mention her preeminence in several non-canonical gospels—are effectively eclipsed. These significant roles, many feminist scholars of religion argue, should garner more attention and lead, not to the position of First Lady of Christianity, but rather to claims about Mary's role as the "first apostle" (Brock).[3] Yet Brown's—and subsequently the popular media and many churches'—fascination with Mary unfortunately revolves around a sexualized notion of her significance, both as wife of Jesus and as embodying the Holy Grail through her womb. Rather than her loyalty and courage (all four canonical gospels place her at the crucifixion of Jesus), bold witness to the resurrection (John 20.11-18), or knowledge of things hidden from the male disciples (Gospel of Mary 6.3-4), Mary's significance is cast in titillating and stereotypical fashion as wife of a powerful man, and as bearer of a royal bloodline. While religious scholarship may benefit from the attention bestowed on Mary Magdalene by Brown's novel, popular conceptions of Mary growing out of *The Da Vinci Code* fail to break out of preconceived notions about why and how women are important agents in religious history.

Still, the deepening investigation into the role of Mary Magdalene in Jesus' life and the life of the early church is an important and significant development in biblical scholarship, and Brown's novel has buoyed this trend. The timing of Karen King's significant book, *The Gospel of Mary of Magdala: Jesus and the First Woman Apostle,* could not have been better. The convergence of Dan

---

[2] Bart Ehrman states, "[I]t is not a narrative Gospel of the type found in the New Testament nor a group of self-contained sayings like the Coptic Gospel of Thomas. It is instead a collection of mystical reflections that have evidently been excerpted from previously existing sermons, treatises, and theological meditations, brought together here under the name of Jesus' disciple, Philip" (*Lost Scriptures* 38).

[3] It is also important to note that the apostolic designation for Mary Magdalene did not originate with contemporary feminists. Rather, second century Hippolytus and fifth century Augustine both referred to Mary as "Apostle to the Apostles" (Morrow).

Brown's novel, King's text and other texts like Elaine Pagels' *Beyond Belief* has not only increased awareness of non-canonical gospels but also helped create openness and curiosity about their contents and their contributions to our understanding of the early church. For instance, through the interpretation of the Gospel of Mary by King and others, we hear that Mary's status as female was not a barrier to spiritual leadership in the ancient church (King 88-9). Further, summer conferences on Mary, such as the one hosted by the all-women Catholic school down the street from my institution, have offered hundreds of *Da Vinci Code* enthusiasts opportunities to expand, deepen and relearn the story of Mary Magdalene and her significance to Jesus and to the early church.

From Mary Magdalene to Sophie Neveu: Sex and the Sacred Feminine

In Brown's novel, the sacred feminine links ancient Mary Magdalene to the contemporary Sophie Neveu, the book's only major female character. Sophie enters the story with bravado, undermining Captain Fache's plans to frame Robert Langdon, and brilliantly orchestrating a get-away for Langdon first from the Louvre and then from Paris altogether. Sophie is clearly in control, and we are privy to Langdon's inner thoughts about her as she successfully dodges authorities: "Langdon decided not to say another word all evening. Sophie Neveu was clearly a hell of a lot smarter than he was" (D. Brown 87). Just as Mary Magdalene appears to upstage Jesus in Brown's story, Sophie seems to intimidate and overpower her Harvard-professor companion; at first blush, female smarts and position seem to represent a version of feminine power that overtakes the power of their male companions.

Or does it? Sophie—known to readers by her first name while her male counterparts are referred to by last names—quickly falls from her vaulted position once she and Langdon arrive at Teabing's estate. Teabing immediately casts Sophie's ignorance of the "true" history of the Grail in an explicitly sexual light: "'Robert, you've brought me a *virgin*? . . . . I thought you were a gentleman. You've robbed her of the climax!' . . . . Teabing already had Sophie locked in his twinkling gaze. 'You are a Grail virgin, my dear. And trust me, you will never forget your first time'" (D. Brown 229). With the exception of solving a riddle on the plane to London, the remainder of the story places Sophie in the role of pupil—or better yet, passive female receptacle—for Langdon and Teabing's vast knowledge of things hidden. She is saved by our hero, and at the story's conclusion, she's clearly got sex on her mind, much to Langdon's surprise.

> "I would love nothing more than to meet you in Florence, Robert. But on *one* condition." Her tone turned serious. "No museums, no churches, no tombs, no art, no relics."
>
> "In Florence? For a week? There's nothing else to do."
>
> Sophie leaned forward and kissed him again, now on the lips. Their bodies came together, softly at first, and then completely. When she pulled away, her eyes were full of promise. (D. Brown 449)

Much like Brown's Mary Magdalene, Sophie initially appears strong, creative, and intelligent; by the end, however, we find her reduced to a sexualized and stereotypical notion of femininity. Brown's heroine, like the iconic Mary Magdalene, embodies a womanhood where significance is determined by and through connection to the male.

Where does all this leave Brown's claims to the power of the sacred feminine? After all, countless women (and men) claim this aspect of the novel is what they appreciate most: the assertion that within Christianity women have laid claim to power, even of the sacred kind. But when we examine what exactly Brown means by the "sacred feminine," the Catholic priest's statement "Brown is really interested in sex" comes again to the fore. Take this passage where Langdon explains the Hieros Gamos ritual to Sophie:

> Historically, intercourse was the act through which the male and female experienced God. The ancients believed that the male was spiritually incomplete until he had carnal knowledge of the sacred feminine. Physical union with the female remained the sole means through which man could become spiritually complete and ultimately achieve *gnosis*—knowledge of the divine. . . . "By communing with woman . . . man could achieve a climactic instant when his mind went totally blank and he could see God." (D. Brown 308-9)

In light of this explanation, can we really accept that Brown's sacred feminine is about the power of women? At the novel's beginning, we hear that Langdon's mission as a symbologist is to help restore the masculine/feminine balance that once held sway in the ancient world. But Langdon's explanation above of the Hieros Gamos tells a different story: we hear that woman is really a vessel for man's physical and spiritual enrichment. In the above passage, the sacred feminine appears to be a sexualized object and tool used by man for his own gain. I would argue that this passage helps reveal Brown's novel for what it is: yet another Grail quest built upon male fantasy that wraps itself in a thin veneer of nobility by cloaking sex in vaguely spiritual terms. Throughout the book, from Mary Magdalene to Sophie to the sacred feminine, the female is ultimately more sexualized than sacralized to fit into Brown's world of women still wanting no more than to be conjoined with their men. From all angles,

Brown's novel fails to live up to its reputation as proffering a feminist version of religion or of restoring any gender balance in male-female relationships.

What's Really Been Covered Up

While Brown ultimately falls short of offering readers a useful or telling glimpse into power of women in ancient Christianity, I want to go further than Dan Brown takes us, beyond the focus on Mary Magdalene and Sophie Neveu, to suggest that the popularity of *The Da Vinci Code* opens an avenue for scholars and church leaders to talk about the role of sexuality in the early church from a very different perspective. Rather than focusing on tantalizing scenarios of a secret marriage, hidden offspring and ancient sex rites, I advocate a turning from Dan to Peter Brown, from the fantastically fictitious to the seriously scholarly exploration of Christianity in antiquity. From his years immersed in the texts and literary fragments of the ancient world, scholar of antiquity Peter Brown insists on the "disturbing strangeness" of the earliest Christians, continuously reminding his readers that ancient Christians had their *backs turned firmly toward us*, and remain (much to Dan Brown's dismay) stubbornly untroubled by our most urgent questions (P. Brown xv, xvii). If we travel with Peter Brown into this strange ancient past, what is perhaps more accurate a cover-up than Mary Magdalene's wifely power is the power of female sexual renunciates and martyrs in the early church. Very unlike a trip into the world of Dan Brown's novel, a journey into the ancient world painted by Peter Brown requires intellectual rigor, patience, and continual suspension of contemporary assumptions about gender, sexuality, and societal expectations. The images of female leadership are more subtle, the glimpses of female power more muted. If we have the patience, however, what is uncovered about women in early Christianity might unexpectedly challenge contemporary assumptions in a way that might even surprise Dan Brown.

Let's travel back to the second century C.E., to Syria, to a radical Christian group called the Encratites. Followers of Tatian, a leader who broke with the Roman church in the second century, members of this group were referred to by others with the term *enkrateia*, or continence, for these Christian men and women abstained from sexual intercourse, and also often from meat and wine. Why the strongly ascetic practices? For the Encratites, the insistence on continence grew out of their particular understanding of the Adamic myth; that is, they understood humanity's perfected state to be without the need for sexual expression. They believed that what was lost in Paradise through the fall was immortality; and when Adam and Eve fell and became mortal, they also became sexually involved with one another. Sex, then, for many Encratites, linked human beings not only to the animal world, but also to the grave. Put bluntly, sex was inextricably bound to death.

From our vantage point and particularly, perhaps, from a feminist perspective, this linking of sex with fallenness rather than with our God-given human nature is highly problematic. Given a choice between the Encratite vision of sexual renunciation as true religious expression and Dan Brown's version of sex as integral to ancient religious practice, most of us might well prefer the New York Times Bestseller version. After all, even Peter Brown himself admits that groups like the Encratites offer a bleak vision of religious devotion (P. Brown 94). But this is where I counsel us to have a little patience, for Peter Brown's chapters average more than three pages each and often do not end with a cliffhanger. If we stay with his analysis of the Encratites a bit longer, we come across this provocative statement: "Yet within this terrible symphony, it is possible to catch a high-pitched refrain of joy and freedom" (P. Brown 95). If we listen closely, Brown suggests, we hear this refrain sung by the Encratites and other continent groups throughout the ancient church of the second century.

To hear the refrain as at all joyful or bespeaking any kind of freedom, it is vital to hear the tune within its second century context. The freedom to which Peter Brown refers is most specifically the freedom experienced by female sexual renunciates. Christian groups like the Encratites offered women a life that departed radically from the expectations of ancient society. In the ancient Roman world, most females wed in their early to mid teens, and were expected to produce as many children as possible for the continuation of society. Marriage, the destiny for virtually all women in antiquity, led to the inevitable enslavement of women to their bodies. As Peter Brown suggests, these women actually lived out the Encratite interpretation of the Adamic myth—they experienced first-hand how sexual intercourse started humanity on a quick and irrevocable journey to the grave. To tie sex so tightly to mortality was likely as much a description of reality to ancient women as it was about an even more ancient creation myth.

With this context in mind, we turn again to the Encratite tradition and its advocacy of continence for both men and women. Becoming part of an ecclesial community like the Encratites entailed being baptized into that particular community. And this baptism within communities such as this literally ushered a person into a new life, one that broke free of worldly bondage to concrete societal expectations. In a world that required bodies to be administered for the perpetuation of society, this "boycott of the womb" by Christian women represented nothing less than a serious affront against the powers-that-be of antiquity. In the words of Peter Brown, "the women's condemnation of the marriage bed was made to stand for all human bondage in the present age, and the rejection of married intercourse, as a window that had suddenly been thrown open to eternity, for [when] 'marriage passeth away with much contempt, Jesus alone abideth'" (Gospel of Thomas qtd. in P. Brown 100). This womb boycott allowed female sexual renunciates like the Encratites to travel the land as missionaries with men, teaching, preaching, and baptizing others in the name of Jesus. These "Holy Ones," as they were called, were proclaiming the death knell of the present age. They saw themselves joining with their bodies in Christ's bodily victory over sin and death.

The longer I work with texts of ancient Christianity and with the interpretative lens of scholars like Peter Brown, the more important I think these stories are for students and practitioners of Christianity to learn about, and to strive to understand. While we should, along with Peter Brown, acknowledge the "terrible" sounds of the symphony of extreme asceticism, I am convinced we must also work to showcase those high-pitched refrains of joy and freedom experienced by groups like the Encratites. In addition, and this is particularly important, getting to the refrain of freedom is essential in addressing the all-too-common critiques of sexual repression and dualism lurking within Christian theology and practice. After all, isn't this part of the reason Dan Brown's story of the cover-up in Christianity resonates so strongly with readers? We want this history to be more about women than it has been, more about the affirmation of bodies and sexuality than it has been. What I have learned from Peter Brown and ancient texts like the Acts of Paul and Thecla, however, is that the renunciation of sex does not necessarily stem from a fundamental hatred of the body or sexuality. Instead, the renunciation of sex and other bodily pleasures grows out of an active defiance of societal claims on human bodies, particularly the female ones. With the introduction of Christian claims that God became a body—and because of this stunning act—bodies no longer need to be merely administered, but can, as with Christ's resurrected body, be transformed. And for those in the ancient world, a central way to transform the body was to eclipse the inevitability of sex and procreation. Careful attention to radical groups like the Encratites offers us unexpected, shockingly egalitarian visions of women who are as capable of bearing the image of God through bodily transformation as are men.

Returning to *The Da Vinci Code*, Dan Brown is right about a cover up of female power and leadership in early Christianity. In the early church there existed powerful—if fleeting—incarnations of the body of Christ where women assumed not only significant leading roles but also participated in destabilizing, embodied upsets of the ancient status quo. I'm not sure Jesus was the original feminist, but I do see that the story of Jesus' life, death, and resurrection opened to women and men radically new ways of living. Dan Brown's novel has contributed to an increasing receptivity to the rich diversity of Christian practices within the ancient world, and has piqued interest in men and women alike about the role of gender and sexuality in Christianity's ancient past. While his portrayal of women fails to teach us much about female power past or present, Dan Brown nevertheless gets people looking for more resources with which to explore these important topics. With the help of scholars like Peter Brown, we can slowly, partially uncover the power held by women in the early church and proclaim it to the church and society, for it has, indeed, been largely lost to contemporary consciousness. In many ways, sexuality is the key, but not at all in the way envisioned by Dan Brown.

Works Cited

Brock, Ann Graham. *Mary Magdalene, The First Apostle: The Struggle for Authority*. Cambridge, Mass: Harvard Theological Studies, Harvard Divinity School: Distributed by Harvard University Press, 2003.

Brooten, Bernadette. Interview. "Speaking of Faith." National Public Radio. 30 January 2004.

Brown, Dan. *The Da Vinci Code*. New York: Random House, 2003.

Brown, Peter. *The Body and Society: Men, Women, and Sexual Renunciation in Early Christianity*. New York: Columbia University Press, 1988.

Ehrman, Bart. *The Lost Christianities: The Battles for Scripture and the Faiths We Never Knew*. Oxford: Oxford UP, 2003

—. *Lost Scriptures: Books That Did Not Make It into the New Testament*. Oxford: Oxford UP, 2003.

King, Karen. *The Gospel of Mary of Magdala: Jesus and the First Woman Apostle*. Santa Rosa, CA: Polebridge Press, 2003.

Morrow, Carol Ann. "Redeeming Her Gospel Reputation." *Catholic Update* May 2006.

Olson, Carl E., and Sandra Miesel. *The Da Vinci Hoax: Exposing the Errors in The Da Vinci Code*. San Francisco: Ignatius Press, 2004.

Pagels, Elaine. *Beyond Belief: The Secret Gospel of Thomas*. New York: Random House, 2003.

Roberts, Roxanne. Interview with Karen King. "The Mysteries of Mary Magdalene: *The Da Vinci Code* Resurrects a Debate of Biblical Proportions." *Washington Post*, 20 July 2003.

CHAPTER THREE

THE "SCHOLAR'S CODE": BIBLICAL INTERPRETATION, POSTMODERNISM, AND *THE DA VINCI CODE*

RACHEL WAGNER, ITHACA COLLEGE

Introduction

The Da Vinci Code has become a crucial prop in contemporary popular debates about epistemology and the Bible. Critics of the novel deal quite explicitly with its implications for biblical interpretation, Christianity, and views about early Christian history. Many Christian critics of the book see its purpose as sinister, intended to destroy the credibility of the Bible and of Christianity. Hank Hanegraaff and Paul Maier identify the novel as part of a "growing movement seeking to reconstruct Christ, reinvent Christianity, and reject the canon of Scripture" (xi). Richard Abanes calls the novel a "well-crafted, cleverly written 454-page diatribe against Christianity" (9). According to Mark Shea and Edward Sri, *The Da Vinci Code* "doesn't have a burning interest in truth"; rather, its claims are "attempts to manipulate us into believing a lie" (45). Indeed, for some Christians, the novel should be construed as "a direct attack against Jesus Christ, the church, and those of us who . . . call him Savior and Lord" (Lutzer xvii). For these Christians, the novel is part of a much larger and malicious cultural movement devoted to undermining the faith of Christians.

Viewing *The Da Vinci Code* within the context of Christian debates about truth, authority, and salvation, I will argue that Brown's novel is important, not for its action-packed adventure tale, but because of the ambivalence about truth and fiction it creates, and the implications this ambivalence has for faith-based readings of the Bible. As I will show, Christian critiques of *The Da Vinci Code* are often presented as a rejection of relativism, which is typically defined rather broadly: Brown's novel, postmodernism, Gnosticism, feminism, and academic historical biblical scholarship all get lumped together as representatives of the same relativistic (and fundamentally "evil") danger. The forces of "good," predictably, are defined as those Christians who adhere to a literalist, faith-based reading of the Bible and decry the dangerous "lies" proposed by Brown in the insidious guise of fiction.

My primary focus is on popular Christian critiques of *The Da Vinci Code*, especially as these critiques deal with biblical interpretation and early Christian history. I include opinions from some of the most popular of these books: *The Gospel Code*, by Ben Witherington III; *Cracking Da Vinci's Code*, by James L. Garlow and Peter Jones; *Breaking The Da Vinci Code*, by Darrell L. Bock; *The Da Vinci Deception*, by Erwin W. Lutzer; *The Da Vinci Code: Fact or Fiction*, by Hank Hanegraaff and Paul L. Maier; *The Da Vinci Deception*, by Mark Shea and Edward Sri; *Cracking Da Vinci's Code*, by Adam Palmer and Jeff Dunn; *The Da Vinci Code: A Quest for Answers*, by Josh McDowell; *The Truth Behind the Da Vinci Code*, by Richard Abanes, and *The Da Vinci Hoax*, by Carl E. Olson and Sandra Miesel. When I generalize about the shared opinions of these authors, I refer to them collectively as "the debunkers."[4]

My goal here is not to endorse or discredit any specific claims about Jesus or Mary Magdalene proffered by the debunkers, by Brown or by his most obvious ideological predecessors, the authors of *Holy Blood, Holy Grail, The Woman with the Alabaster Jar,* and *The Templar Revelation.*[5] Nor will I discuss Brown's theories about Leonardo da Vinci, the Priory of Sion, Opus Dei, any of the material relating to art history or legends of the Holy Grail. Instead, I will deal with Christian responses to the popularization of academic biblical criticism associated with *The Da Vinci Code*, especially insofar as these critical approaches are perceived as a threat to traditional Christianity and faith-based forms of biblical interpretation. I end by showing how some Christian theologians today reject this reactive stance toward postmodernism and argue instead that postmodernism can serve as the foundation of a richer form of biblical interpretation.

---

[4] I am especially interested in the *kinds* of arguments being made by these authors, so the focus is topical rather than a rehearsal of each author's individual argument. This means that to some extent, the fine distinctions between the authors will be dulled. Catholic and Protestant, evangelical and self-identified fundamentalist, are all sifted through to see what kinds of arguments crop up repeatedly, by self-proclaimed Christians, with the professed aim of debunking *The Da Vinci Code*. Those readers interested in the nuances of exactly how individual faith traditions affect specific authors' views should read these authors' books in their entirety.

[5] Respectively, these are Michael Baigent, Richard Leigh, and Henry Lincoln (New York: Dell Books), 1982; Margaret Starbird (Rochester, Vermont: Bear & Company), 1993; and Lynn Picknett and Clive Prince (New York: Simon and Schuster), 1997.

"Phony" Facts, "Perverted" Fiction, and Biblical Interpretation

The Da Vinci Code is baffling to many Christians precisely *because* it blurs the distinction between fact and fiction, frustrating those who proclaim their own beliefs about Jesus and the gospel accounts of his life to be "fact." Garlow and Jones worry that Christians who read the novel may become "confused about just who Jesus really is" and as a result turn "away from what they thought to be true to grasp a mangled mass of bizarre claims cleverly portrayed as a work of history in a work of fiction" (23). Witherington agrees, grieving that "in our postmodern culture, where Jesus is a household name but most people are biblically illiterate, almost anything can pass as the truth about the historical Jesus" (144). Shea and Sri worry that Christian readers of Brown's novel may ask: "Is Christianity one gigantic and audacious lie? Has all of Western civilization been founded on the biggest fraud in history?" (3).

The consternation the novel has created is readily evident in the ways that debunkers describe its confusion of categories: Garlow and Jones scathingly label Brown's novel "fact-ion" (58). Allen complains that the novel is filled with "phony 'facts'" (3). Hanegraaff and Maier woefully opine that "[f]iction—such as the notion that Christianity was concocted to subjugate women—is being cleverly peddled as fact—while fact—such as the deity of Christ—is being capriciously passed off as fiction" (viii). Demonstrating the confusion that the fact/fiction debate has caused, Shea and Sri offer the odd-sounding dictum that "[f]iction is great when it is told in order to speak the truth. Fiction is perverted and evil when it is told in order to speak lies" (4). Christians, they explain, should reject *The Da Vinci Code* because it is "precisely what Brown claims the Christian story to be: a fiction invented in order to support an ideology, full of events that did not happen" (119). The popularization of previously little known academic approaches to biblical interpretation, along with the mainstreaming of certain aspects of postmodern philosophy, have resulted in what Garlow and Jones call the potential loss of "objective truth," without which "we have nothing solid to hold onto" (25).

Through its confusion of fact and fiction, *The Da Vinci Code* has made biblical interpreters of every reader, bringing in its wake an avalanche of associated books filled with information about the methods of biblical interpretation. The debunkers' responses to biblical scholars' methods of historical interpretation constitute the "Scholar's Code."[6]

---

[6] Darrell Bock uses this term in *Breaking The Da Vinci Code* to refer to the historical arguments of scholars like Elaine Pagels, Karen King, and the Jesus Seminar, presenting them as a misleading "code" to be broken by the faithful Christian. The "Scholars'

The "Scholars' Code"

In *The Da Vinci Code*, the hero is Robert Langdon, a Harvard professor of "symbology." Through his wits and verve, Langdon is able, nearly single-handedly, to solve the mystery of the code, all in his stylish tweed jacket, unruffled and encyclopedic in his brilliance. Langdon is also a skeptic about organized religion. Indeed, some might argue that it is precisely this skepticism that enables him to succeed in his quest, since he is readily willing to doubt the received Christian interpretation of biblical history and embrace a radically new and dangerous reading of the same biblical history.

In contrast to the heroic characterization of Robert Langdon, in the writings of the debunkers of *The Da Vinci Code* real-life academics tend to get a fairly bad rap. Peter Jones describes his graduate career in religious studies at Harvard, where he was confronted by a "roomful of Langdons" who "were committed to undermining the faith [Peter] held dear" (Garlow and Jones 131). He dismally observes that what he labels "liberal religious scholarship" is no longer "hidden away in dry, dusty tomes on university library shelves" but has "burst into view in an attractive novel and . . . in an action-packed movie" (132). Jones grieves the popularization of academic biblical interpretation: "Now everyone who has read *The Da Vinci Code* has learned what I learned in the academic world thirty-some years ago" (132).

What most offends the debunkers is the academic assumption that, at least for the purposes of historical analysis, the Bible can and should be viewed as a product of human beings. According to this view, the Bible should be read alongside other ancient non-canonical documents, which are to be viewed as fellow witnesses to the diversity of early Christian belief. By suggesting that early Christian history is more characterized by diversity than by unity, biblical historians often find themselves the target of those Christians with a stake in claiming the Bible is a vessel of singular and undisputed "truth." By viewing the Bible in this way, Maier claims, the Scholars are "attempting to ruin the historical disciplines" (39).

For many of the debunkers, Brown's claims call into question the very nature of Jesus, suggesting that he was not divine but was "merely a mortal man," so that "the heart is ripped out of the good news of Christianity and the Bible is not worth the paper it's written on" (Garlow and Jones 85). They worry that, after reading *The Da Vinci Code*, Christians will doubt "the actual, literal, physical resurrection of Jesus" and will replace the Bible, transplanting faith with "learning theology from a novel" (72, 82).

Code," Bock claims, is "where the novel and scholarship converge" in their troubling attempts to dismantle the received tradition of early Christian history (101).

The issue then, is not so much the novel *itself*, but rather what the novel demands of its readers in terms of their reading of the Bible. By introducing ordinary readers to basic questions of biblical history, canonization, and diversity of early Christian belief, the novel requires any reader wishing to make sense of the novel's claims to also learn more about the development of the Bible in its historical context. This means that they must also decide which biblical scholars they trust, and on what grounds. The *real* mystery, then, is not so much what happened to Saunière or with what conspiracies Opus Dei may or may not be involved. The mystery to be solved is *how* we know *what* we know about Jesus, about the Bible, and about the development of the early church. When we understand this to be the real question lurking behind the novel, the question of its immense popularity comes into sharper focus. The problem, in short, is epistemological, and the debate is quickly taking shape as a conflict of assumptions between the faith-based reading of the debunkers and the historical methods of the Scholars.

Walter Bauer's well-known thesis about the complexity of early Christianity, nuanced and popularized by scholars like Bart Erhman, Elaine Pagels, and the scholars of the Jesus Seminar, stands in stark contrast to the traditional view.[7] This traditional view, sanctioned by the debunkers, posits that Christian orthodoxy "follows a straight line from the teaching of Jesus in the thirties to the writings of Paul and the other apostles in the latter half of the first century, to the final decrees of the ecumenical synods in the fifth century, seeking to preserve this original unique truth" (Garlow and Jones 151). By contrast, biblical scholars like Ehrman and Pagels propose that early Christianity was a stew of competing forms of practice and belief, and the Bible, properly read, provides a window into this early diversity. When one considers also the apocryphal texts of the New Testament period and the new evidence provided by the discovery of the Nag Hammadi texts, then the argument for complexity is difficult to ignore.

Although most of the Scholars' research has little to do with *The Da Vinci Code* debate, scholars like Elaine Pagels, Karen King, Marcus Borg, James Robinson, and Bart Ehrman have found themselves repeatedly referenced in popular discussions about biblical interpretation that have spilled over from the novel.[8] For example, Ben Witherington III accuses Elaine Pagels, Karen King,

---

[7] See Walter Bauer, *Orthodoxy and Heresy in Earliest Christianity* (Philadelphia: Fortress Press), 1971.

[8] See especially Elaine Pagels, *The Gnostic Gospels* (New York: Vintage Press), 1989; *Beyond Belief: The Secret Gospel of Thomas* (New York: Vintage Press), 2003; Karen King, *What is Gnosticism?* (Cambridge, MA: Belknap Press), 2003; Marcus Borg, *Reading the Bible Again for the First Time* (Harper San Francisco), 2002; *Meeting Jesus Again for the First Time* (Harper San Francisco), 1995; James Robinson, ed. *The Nag*

and scholars "like them" of having "been burned" by orthodox Christianity. The Scholars have, in his opinion, "creat[ed] a new myth of Christian origins, one that better suits their own more human-centered approaches to religion" and one which the debunkers believe has some central features in common with *The Da Vinci Code* (95). Garlow and Jones concur, claiming that Elaine Pagels was once an "evangelical Christian," but is now on a "similar mission" as Dan Brown: to discredit traditional Christianity and its view of early church history (169). Bart Ehrman "plows the same furrow as Pagels and King," engaging in "revisionist history writing" and arguing for "the very same sort of wide diversity of beliefs" as Pagels and King believe characterized early Christianity (122-3).

Witherington's most pronounced ire is reserved for Marcus Borg, to whom he devotes an entire chapter. As one of the most well known members of the Jesus Seminar project, Borg is a favorite target of critics of *The Da Vinci Code*, who see his worldview as consistent with Brown's novel, despite the fact that neither he, Pagels, nor King have written directly about the novel at all. For the debunkers, Brown's views are consistent with those of the Jesus Seminar, "who are committed to the undermining of biblical Christianity" (Garlow and Jones 87).

This, then, is the crucial link between Borg and Brown—both call into question the traditional reading of the gospel, specifically a reading of the miracles as literally true. Borg, then, can be seen as a kindred spirit to Brown, and can be dismissed for the same reasons that Pagels and King are dismissed. By acknowledging the complexity of early Christianity, the Scholars deny its unity, an act that for Witherington is tantamount to dismissing the Bible as a credible source of truth.

Hammadi Library (Harper San Francisco), 1990; Bart Ehrman, *Lost Christianities* (Oxford: Oxford University Press), 2003. In response to a request from his editor, Ehrman even wrote a book exclusively about *The Da Vinci Code: Truth and Fiction in The Da Vinci Code* (Oxford University Press, 2004). Darrell Bock's *Breaking The Da Vinci Code*, although theologically consistent with many of the views of the debunkers, is in some ways distinctive, since it does present a sympathetic portrayal of Elaine Pagels' scholarly work on Gnosticism, even as Bock disagrees with the implications of her scholarship (Bock 65). For example, Bock praises Pagels' *The Gnostic Gospels*, and acknowledges that Gnosticism should be studied for the insights it provides us about the "division in the Christian house of faith of the first three centuries" (86). However, he claims that Pagel's analysis of Gnosticism reflects an "agenda," i.e. "to revise [the] orthodox faith" through "the rejection of Christian faith as a historically unified set of core beliefs held over the centuries starting from the earliest period" (88-9). In effect, the more sympathetic Pagels' portrayal of Gnosticism is, the more readily she can be identified as a proponent of Gnosticism, seeking to dethrone the orthodox traditional beliefs about early Christianity.

Witherington's dispute here is theological, not historical; nobody is questioning the existence of many texts that reflect competing beliefs about Jesus; the issue is about the authority of these texts and their relationship to the Bible. For Witherington and the other debunkers, the academic argument for diversity in early Christianity is disputed on a *faith-based* assumption of church unity and on a *faith-based* conviction that the Bible stands alone in comparison to other ancient texts as the only perfect vessel for "truth."

So who has the proper credentials with which to interpret the Bible and assess its authority, and thus also the credentials with which to confront the challenges posed by *The Da Vinci Code*? Richard Abanes, writing as a Christian (and as an academic) critical of what he sees as *The Da Vinci Code*'s irresponsible representation of early Christianity, objects to the credentials of the authors of the four leading reference works utilized by Brown:

> [Margaret] Starbird [(*The Woman with the Alabaster Jar*)] holds an M.A. in comparative literature and German. [Michael] Baigent [(*Holy Blood, Holy Grail*)] has an undergraduate degree in psychology and has recently been pursuing an M.A. in Mysticism and Religious Experience. And [Richard] Leigh [(*Holy Blood, Holy Grail*)] "is primarily a novelist and writer of short stories." What about [Henry] Lincoln [(*Holy Blood, Holy Grail*)]? He is a BBC television personality and scriptwriter. And [Lynn] Picknett and Clive Prince [(*The Templar Revelation*)] are actually conspiracy theorists with a penchant for occultism, the paranormal, and UFOs. (41-42)

For Abanes, the sources to which Brown turns are themselves of questionable authority, written by people who have neither the academic nor the theological credentials with which to propose viable theories about the early church. Nor, as we have seen, do the debunkers trust the opinions of the Scholars, who they claim operate at "some of the most prestigious institutions in the United States" and use their influence "on national TV and in magazines" in "a conscious effort to obscure the uniqueness and vitality of the Christian faith and message" (Bock 155, 95).

Bock allows his critique of Brown's novel to spill over into his critique of the Scholars, since he suggests that the "best-selling novel" has simply "elaborated on and embellished these more academic ideas" (156). Francis Moloney sees the novel as "flying on the coattails" of the "scholarly activities" of people like Pagels, King, and the Jesus Seminar, since they too call into question the traditional view of a unified early Christianity (xviii). In what amounts to an argument of guilt by association, Bock, Moloney, and other debunkers condemn and reject the work of the Scholars, most of whom have never even commented on *The Da Vinci Code*.

The dispute, then, is much larger than what happened to Jesus and when; it is even much larger than *The Da Vinci Code* itself, or even than the critiques of it issued by the debunkers. The cultural debate we are now engaged in is about how we know what we know, who has the right or the authority to teach it to us, and what role, if any, faith should play in that knowledge. As I explore below, postmodernism has become a catch-all term to apply not only to the opinions of the Scholars, but also to what the debunkers see as multiple threats to faith-based convictions about the Bible and its "truth."

Postmodernism: The "New Gnosticism"?

For the debunkers, Brown's novel is more than just a work of fiction; it is a tract "making a case for an old form of spirituality that is reappearing in the twentieth century" (Garlow and Jones 179). Garlow and Jones ominously remark: "Gnostic texts are flying off bookstore shelves faster than they can be stocked" (168). Palmer and Dunn see *The Da Vinci Code* as a "call to return to Gnosticism," a trend they see reflected in "many movies and books" that are "all around us" (99). The Gnostic worldview, Erwin Lutzer claims, is roughly equivalent to relativism; it "is broad enough to embrace our culture and lets us believe pretty much whatever we want to believe" (20).

As a result, the debunkers define modern Gnosticism in exceedingly broad ways; Garlow and Jones' laundry list of modern Gnostics include: "The East with its gurus, its spirituality, and its yoga," members of the controversial Jesus Seminar, feminists, proponents of liberal sexuality, in short, anything that challenges their own traditional view of Christianity, usually through arguing for the importance of individual perspective in interpretation. Viewing the recent popularization of the Gnostic writings found at Nag Hammadi as particularly ominous, Garlow and Jones assert:

> These Gnostic writings have reappeared at a time when patriarchy, doctrinal precision, canons, confessions, clearly defined sexual morality, church institutions, and authority are out. What's in? The personal spiritual quest, diversity, individualism, egalitarianism, and sexual liberation. And the prospect of finding ancient "Christian" scrolls[9] that support this new era's spiritual viewpoint is, for many postmoderns, a dream come true. (168)

According to the debunkers, then, Gnosticism and postmodernism are essentially synonymous–as are Eastern religions, paganism, multiculturalism,

---

[9] The authors appear to be referring primarily to the Nag Hammadi Gnostic texts, which were recorded not on scrolls, but on codices. Interestingly, Dan Brown makes the same error, causing one to wonder if Garlow and Jones have acquired some of their information, however faulty, from Brown rather than from original research. See Brown 234 and Ehrman 26.

goddess worship, and a whole host of other phenomena, all of which acknowledge the crucial role of individual perspective in determining truth. This spirituality, they argue, takes on a plethora of forms but at root "the postmoderns" are united in their rejection of absolute truth (181). Garlow and Jones identify two possible worldviews: "There might be hundreds of factions (religions) with their unique little agendas, but ultimately they will all eventually align themselves under two fundamental alliances: pagan monism and biblical theism" (223).[10] The former is the enemy of Christian faith; the latter is the remedy for doubt.

Any perspective that emphasizes the importance of human experience above the teachings of traditional church authority is suspect. In a vein consistent with recent fundamentalist concerns about Harry Potter, Garlow and Jones argue that *The Da Vinci Code* is of a type with *The Craft*, *Charmed*, *Sabrina the Teenage Witch*, and other pop culture iterations of witchcraft (204). Similarly, Palmer and Dunn urge careful Christian consumers to be wary of the "Gnostic influence" of the "enemy" reflected in films like *The Matrix, Star Wars,* and *Minority Report* (98-99). For these debunkers, *The Da Vinci Code* is just the most recent and dangerous symptom of an insidious resurfacing of the ancient Gnostic "heresy." Dan Brown is "casting a spell over his readers" and "lulls them into a dreamlike state where they will stop believing in the real world and come to live forever in a dungeon" (108). To reject the novel's slippery, if fictitious, temptations is for these debunkers tantamount to rejecting the dark forces of sorcery and witchcraft.

The Scholars, too, are accused of being mistakenly in tune with postmodern and/or Gnostic forces. By viewing the New Testament texts within their historical context and arguing for the diversity of early Christianity, Witherington sees the Scholars recycling the Gnostic worldview in a distinctively dangerous and clever form:

> If there is no ultimate authority when it comes to truth, then people are free to make their own truth. This is, in the end, what the old Gnostics did long ago, and history is repeating itself. It seems clear to me that this is what happened to some of these scholars. Because they relativize the Bible's authority, they have no problem with putting their own ideas in its place. We are witnessing the oldest kind of intellectual sin being re-committed in the newest kinds of ways. These scholars . . . are oblivious to the fact that they are being led down this path by the powers of darkness. (174)

---

[10] This dualistic perspective also has the interesting effect of minimizing doctrinal differences between Catholics and Protestants, insofar as there are many Christians from both traditions who argue for apostolic tradition as the most reliable criterion for "truth" of the Bible, even if they do not clearly articulate what it means to speak of the Bible's "truth."

Witherington and his fellow debunkers consider the Gnostic worldview, the perspective of these academic scholars, and postmodernism to be cut from the same portentous cloth. The Scholars, having "freed themselves from biblical orthodoxy, are on a similar mission" as the proponents of other forms of relativism, namely to destroy the faith of Christians (168-9).

Witherington's rejection of Borg's views is not grounded in a careful analysis of the disputed gospel passages, but rather is based on an accusation of moral relativism: "Borg doesn't seem to realize that when we make experience the ultimate guide, we have to be able to distinguish between good and bad, helpful and unhelpful, enlightening and deceiving experience" (132). Maier suggests that Dan Brown too may be "post-[m]odernist in his philosophy" since he appears to ascribe to the belief that "whatever is true for you is the truth, pure and simple; there are no objective standards or universal norms, since everything is relative" (39). Despite the lack of clarity that many of the debunkers reflect about postmodernism, it does seem evident that their concerns are not just about *The Da Vinci Code*, and not even just about the historical questions the novel raises, but rather are part of a much larger anxiety about epistemology, especially as it relates to religious belief and salvation.

The Debunkers' Warning

In response to the threat of postmodernism, Garlow and Jones advise that Christians should "keep all [their] wits about [them] in this debate about truth" (170). For those Christians with the proper faith stance, the crisis of truth should be of no concern since Jesus "unabashedly calls Himself the sole source of truth" (210). McDowell counters Brown's Robert Langdon with the creation of a fictional history professor of his own, and reassures his Christian readers through her that some (Christian) people "just seem to have an ear for the truth" (44).[11] Referring to the famous passage in John (14:6)[12], Garlow and Jones propose that "there *is* such a thing as an absolute, knowable truth," and

---

[11] Indeed, McDowell adds, the choices one makes about "truth" and "history" are of eternal importance, since "according to the historical record, Jesus apparently thought it was critical what others believed about him. It was not a subject that allowed for neutrality" (86). As McDowell's character Andrea explains at the end of his book, the real issue is submission to God and a plea for his forgiveness, because "this isn't about people who lived two thousand years ago, or even about a code created by a renaissance genius; it's about—well, it's about me" (90). Reflecting the stark dualism so typical of the debunkers, Andrea then rejects Brown's novel and embraces Christianity.

[12] "Jesus said to [Thomas], 'I am the way, and the truth, and the life; no one comes to the Father, but by me.'"

Christians have access to it–not through rational argumentation, but through faith alone, with the Bible as the window of access to this "truth" (211).

Nonetheless, the danger of relativism is palpable to the debunkers, who see themselves as spiritual warriors, "warning" readers that "real demons can deceive and influence" readers (202). Lutzer agrees that readers can easily be deceived, and that we are "engaged in nothing less than a battle for the real Bible" (22). Brown has told "malicious lies" in order "to attack the Gospel of Jesus Christ and replace it with a resurgent pagan mythos" (Allen 3). Wary Christian readers should not rely upon their own interpretive devices, but rather should put their trust in "revelation," which undercuts the relativism of our world in its divine origins (Garlow and Jones 170).

The debunkers' Christian worldview is decidedly dualistic, with distinctive apocalyptic overtones: the world as divided between forces of good and forces of evil, and every cultural item, every ideological stance, every academic theory can be aligned with one force or the other.[13] It could be argued, then, that how readers respond to *The Da Vinci Code* is a fair litmus test of his or her status in salvation. To the debunkers, *The Da Vinci Code* is "an ideological call to arms" and the "code" that it offers is a demonic threat (Allen 3).

This dualistic view is comprehensive: Eastern religions, Gnosticism, and postmodernism are representations of the forces of evil precisely because they *reject* the dualism of good and evil, and attempt to "join the opposites" (Garlow and Jones 207). The "pagan view of the world" supported in *The Da Vinci Code*, Garlow and Jones claim, denies dualism altogether and *in so doing* identifies itself *as* evil (209). *The Da Vinci Code*, then, far from being an innocent piece of fictional fluff, is a billboard for relativism, fighting for the souls of believers in a spiritual war of cosmic proportions. The strange argument for a *dualism* that identifies *monism* as evil is a hallmark of the debunkers' theology.

The debunkers' most popular means of confronting the relativism of the postmodern worldview is to posit truth in a supernatural realm. God is described "outside the circle" of the material, human world (Garlow and Jones 224). God "has His own place, His own domain of existence" (225). Our world may indeed be a global melting pot of beliefs, but the "truth" that transcends this chaos, i.e. God, is utterly removed from it. The Bible, for these Christians, is the divine window through which we can view this certainty from within the context of our messy world. The Christian response to *The Da Vinci Code*, then, should be the same as the Christian response to postmodernism, Eastern religions, feminism, liberal sexuality, and historical biblical scholarship: all of these should be

[13] Interestingly, one may convincingly argue that the debunkers' dualism sounds much like a new form of Manichaeism, a starkly dualistic tradition with many similarities to Gnosticism, and one of the early church's main threats.

soundly rejected as modern manifestations of the ancient heresy of Gnosticism, and more importantly, as spiritual threats.

The "New Reformers": Making Peace with Postmodernism

Not all Christians take the route of the debunkers and demonize postmodernism; on the contrary, some new theologians, whom I dub the "New Reformers," claim that postmodernism is the friend of faith. Furthermore, these theologians resist the temptation to lump postmodernism together with any ideology that offends traditional Christianity and instead, try to take postmodern philosophy seriously, then apply its insights to their own faith-based perspectives. Consequently, their arguments are more concerned with the questions raised by *The Da Vinci Code* than with the novel itself.

Building his case for a new approach to Christian theology, evangelical theologian Carl Raschke claims that Christianity "made [an] unholy alliance with Cartesian rationalism and British evidentialism as far back as the seventeenth century" (9). The loss of faith that characterizes much of modern Christianity, Raschke claims, heralds the need for a new Reformation. As if responding directly to the debunkers, Raschke suggests that evangelicalism has "unwittingly succumbed to the kind of facile and expedient rationalism that the Reformers had valiantly exposed in Catholic doctrine and sought to expunge from the practice of the Christian faith" (30).

Today, the problem is intensified, since postmodernism has "begun to pound at the door of evangelical thought and faith" (11). Should evangelicals let it in, Raschke asks? Whereas the debunkers respond, "Absolutely not!" Raschke's enthusiastic reply is: "Yes!" Despite the bad rap postmodernism has gotten, as "an outlook and habit of thinking that fosters nihilism, moral relativism, as well as emotionalism and irrationalism," Raschke claims that postmodernism is actually the friend of evangelicalism, since it encourages the dismissal of the unhealthy partnership between rationalism and biblical interpretation that so pervades much of modern evangelical Christianity. Instead of looking for external verification of scripture, Raschke argues, evangelicals should embrace the insights of postmodernists like Jean Baudrillard, Emmanuel Lévinas and Maurice Blanchot. Fighting what Doug Groothuis calls "truth decay," Raschke wants to use postmodernism to argue for the transcendence of truth itself, and views the Bible as a tool that points beyond itself to a God who cannot be contained within it (15).

Although this gesture toward transcendence sounds at first like the arguments of the debunkers, Raschke's case is altogether different, since earthly relativism is, for him, not a threat but an invitation to faith. In other words, the apocalyptic dualism is replaced with a Joban acknowledgment of the mystery of

God's transcendence. By embracing the indeterminacy of texts—even the biblical tex—the suggests that evangelical Christians can shed the obligation to the Cartesian model of truth acquisition that "hard-core Christian rationalists" cling to, and replace it with a faith based on experience, accepting of the incompleteness of human perspective which in turn opens the door to the humility of faith in a God-centered perspective (20). In short, he argues that postmodernism opens up evangelical theology by putting the element of sheer faith back into it, and all without demonizing popular culture, academic scholarship, or religious pluralism.

For Raschke, postmodernism is the ideal means by which to achieve this return to faith, since by "calling attention to the finite boundaries of human knowledge and meaning," postmodernism makes it possible for God to "continue to speak and disclose himself from his infinite throne on high" (31). The parabolic nature of scripture seems, for Raschke, to confirm the need for such an approach. Whereas "it would be gratuitous to call Jesus a postmodernist," Raschke wryly observes that "it should give us pause that his contemporaries put him down for many of the same grievances for which some attack postmodernists today" (20).

Mimicking the Protestant Reformation's call for a return to scripture and faith, Raschke's "Next Reformation" urges a return "to the Word not as a logical construct, but as the living power and presence" of God (33). The new Reformation, drawing on the insights of postmodernist philosophy, will create a "dynamic new relational faith." Postmodernism, precisely by "relativizing language and the theories of signification, . . . makes it possible to honor *the immeasurable holiness* of God" (32). Rejecting traditional "theistic representations" of God, Raschke draws on Derrida to assert that when we "speak of God, we warp and raddle texts, yet the presence of God is not to be experienced in the text per se, but in the 'margins,' 'holes,' and 'gaps' that surround and penetrate the text" (58). Applying what one might call a postmodern form of negative theology, Raschke uses Derrida to tear down the text, arguing that faith allows God to remain when the text has fallen apart.

Using the analogy of the Eucharist, Raschke cautions his readers that the text is only a sign pointing to a greater truth: "The significance of [the Gospels] arises from what we say about the text, how we . . . 'deconstruct' it . . . [how we] disassemble it, to rend it into pieces as Christ was torn apart on the cross" (90). Here Raschke departs from Derrida and the deconstructionists, turning the apparent nihilism of deconstructionism on its head: "If, as Derrida has intimated, there is nothing 'outside' the text then the sacred text is the same as sacred presence . . . 'Salvation' can be found in 'dying' to our representations and being born anew as readers" (90). Raschke's move is slick and almost imperceptible; claiming to reject the Platonic view of truth (and of God) as transcendent to creation, Raschke argues for an incarnational approach to scripture that is shaped and determined in time by real readers.

Gene Edward Veith offers a similar appeal to a transcendent God as a means of dealing with the threat of postmodernism:

> Without a belief in God. . . it would be difficult to avoid the postmodernist conclusions [of "intellectual relativism"]. If there is no transcendental logos, then there can be no absolutes, no meaning apart from human culture, no way out of the prison house of language. Such postmodern theories may represent the ultimate development of secular thought—skepticism turning upon itself, human autonomy discovering its own impotence. Postmodernism may represent the dead-end—the implosion, the deconstruction—of human attempts to do without God. (68)

For Veith, postmodernism can serve as a step toward God, since it exposes the limits of reason and the "arrogance of the Enlightenment" (68). Christians who use the insights of postmodernism to expose the limitations of human reasoning will be rewarded with the gift of faith, which steps in when postmodernism fails. In other words, he proposes that postmodernism deconstructs our human confidence in what we know, and leaves space in which faith alone can act. He explains: "The Bible, like the postmodernists, advocates the death of the self. But unlike the postmodernists, the Bible promises a redemption and resurrection of the self" (87).

For Raschke, Veith, and other Christian theologians like them, a perspective-based reading of the Bible is essential precisely because it points to the incompleteness and the indeterminacy of the text of the Bible in favor of a completeness and a determinacy in the divine realm.[14] Whether this Christian-postmodernist attempt to unite relativism and absolute "truth" is a contradiction in terms or a mystery of faith is impossible to demonstrate. But it is clear that these theologians are attempting to use the deconstruction of rational meaning so basic to the postmodernist enterprise to rally a call for faith as a replacement for relativism. In so doing, they offer a means of dealing with the challenges of today's society and provocative popular culture items like *The Da Vinci Code* without closing themselves off in an angry and reactive posture.

---

[14] For a more complete discussion of some of the most pressing issues relating to Christianity and postmodernism by a variety of modern theologians, see Myron B. Penner, ed., *Christianity and the Postmodern Turn* (Grand Rapids, Michigan: Brazos Press), 2005 and Kevin J. Vanhoozer, ed., *The Cambridge Companion to Postmodern Theology* (Cambridge: Cambridge University Press), 2003.

Conclusion

The debunkers and the "New Reformation" Christians must all deal with the challenges raised by postmodernism. All must deal with the troubling but persistent question of what is "fact" and what is "fiction" in the biblical accounts of Jesus' life. All must face the challenge of the increasing role of the individual in biblical interpretation, and all must determine what role personal experience can and should play in this process. Both the debunkers and the "New Reformers" appeal to a supernatural Godhead whose authority is not affected by the chaos of a postmodern world. However, the means by which they appeal to this God differ significantly.

The debunkers define postmodernism very broadly, lumping together any ideology, any practice, or any viewpoint that utilizes individual experience as a crucial component in determining meaning. Thus, they can put academic biblical historians, feminists, practitioners of eastern religions, and readers of *The Da Vinci Code* all in the same boat. All are simultaneously charged with moral and/or epistemological relativism. In defying what the debunkers view as the "truth" of Christianity (as they see it), these "postmoderns" are identified as opponents in a spiritual war. Debunking *The Da Vinci Code*, then, is not just an intellectual or a spiritual exercise, but it is an act of faith in a spiritual battle being waged for the souls of all human beings.

The "New Reformers," however, offer a more nuanced stance toward postmodernism, suggesting that postmodern philosophy does Christianity a favor by pointing out what is missing: namely, the "truth" that they claim God offers believers. By dismantling the view that Christianity can and should be "proven," the New Reformers see postmodernism as leveling the ground in preparation for the building up of faith. Both groups claim that in our contemporary world, it is exceedingly difficult to determine what is "truth" and what is "fiction." However, whereas the debunkers insist that the Bible offers a clear and accessible template for Christian belief and practice, and thus are comfortable identifying the "enemies" to their faith, for the New Reformers the Bible points beyond itself to God, who is always more than humans can possibly conceive. Whereas the debunkers demonize their opponents, the New Reformers forge a new direction for Christian theology, and in so doing, offer what may be one of the most promising Christian responses to the epistemological challenges of *The Da Vinci Code*.

All readers will have to muddle through this new phase in the history of biblical interpretation, including those who self-identify as Christians and those who do not. The Postmodern Reformation is upon us, and easy theology will no longer satisfy most people, who can introduce themselves to a hundred different opinions about biblical interpretation with the click of a mouse.[15] Scholars like Marcus Borg, Elaine Pagels, and Bart Ehrman will not be silenced by accusations of being in league with dark forces, nor will most readers be easily dissuaded from reading them or *The Da Vinci Code* on such charges. Instead, we must all become comfortable with our new roles as reformers, whether we choose to accept the received traditions of a particular thread of Christianity or cast off into new interpretive waters, propelled forward only by our desire to know more.

Works Cited

Abanes, Richard. *The Truth Behind The Da Vinci Code.* Eugene, OR: Harvest House Publishers, 2004.

Allen, Tom. "Introduction." *The Da Vinci Deception.* Mark Shea and Edward Sri. West Chester, PA: Ascension Press, 2006.

Bock, Darrell. *Breaking The Da Vinci Code.* Nashville, Tennessee: Nelson Books, 2004.

Ehrman, Bart D. *Truth and Fiction in The Da Vinci Code.* Oxford: Oxford University Press, 2004.

Garlow, James L. and Peter Jones. *Cracking Da Vinci's Code.* Colorado Springs, Co: Cook Communications Ministries, 2004.

Hanegraaff, Hank and Paul L. Maier. *The Da Vinci Code: Fact or Fiction?* Wheaton, Illinois: Tyndale House Publishers, 2004.

Lutzer, Erwin W. *The Da Vinci Deception.* Wheaton, Illinois: Tyndale House Publishers, 2004.

McDowell, Josh. *The Da Vinci Code: A Quest for Answers.* Holiday, Florida: Green Key Books, 2006.

Moloney, Francis J. "Foreword." *Breaking The Da Vinci Code.* Darrell Bock. Nashville, Tennessee: Nelson Books, 2004.

Olson, Carl E. and Sandra Miesel. *The Da Vinci Hoax.* San Francisco: Ignatius Press, 2004.

Palmer, Adam and Jeff Dunn. *Cracking Da Vinci's Code: The Hidden Agenda Unveiled.* Colorado Springs, CO: Cook Communications Ministries, 2006.

---

[15] The term "Postmodern Reformation" was coined by Leonard Sweet, Dean of the Theological School and professor of postmodern Christianity at Drew University in New Jersey. However, Sweet's use of the term is grounded in his personal call for the church to become "postmodern," so that it can "kiss Howard Stern," and so its worship "meets the 'wow' standard" (20, 44). For Sweet, the church must be "awakened to a postmodern world open to revelation and hungry for experience" (29). See *Postmodern Pilgrims: First Century Passion for the Twenty-First Century World* (Nashville, TN: Broadman & Holman Publishers), 2000.

Raschke, Carl. *The Next Reformation: Why Evangelicals Must Embrace Postmodernity.* Cedar Rapids, MI: Baker Academic, 2004.

Shea, Mark and Edward Sri. *The Da Vinci Deception.* West Chester, PA: Ascension Press, 2006.

Veith, Gene Edward. *Postmodern Times: A Christian Guide to Contemporary Thought and Culture.* Wheaton, Illinois: Crossway Books, 1994.

Williams, Gary. *The Da Vinci Code: From Dan Brown's Fiction to Mary Magdalene's Faith.* Geanies House, Fearn, Tain, Ross-shire, Scotland: Christian Focus Publications, 2006.

Witherington, Ben, III. *The Gospel Code: Novel Claims about Jesus, Mary Magdalene, and Da Vinci.* Downer's Grove, Illinois: InterVarsity Press, 2004.

CHAPTER FOUR

EXPERIENCING IS BELIEVING: THE FEMININE DIVINE EXPOSED

ARLETTE POLAND, CLAREMONT GRADUATE UNIVERSITY

What we personally experience in life tells us much of what we need to discern regarding what is real and true for us. When we experience the deity—God, Allah, YHWH, or Brahman—as a male, that is our truth because that is our experience. As we mature in life, it behooves us to question our assumptions and beliefs to ensure that they are still true for us, personally. We can ask questions of ourselves such as "Is this really true for me have I accepted it from some other source and allowed it to be my truth without questioning the source or my own experience?" Such questioning is typically the ambit of science, philosophy and theology. We place our experiences, and so our beliefs, under other people's personal or professional authority, when it might better serve us to also do this with our own beliefs and perspectives. Who says truth has to be the same for everyone? If that were the case, then there wouldn't be such variety and diversity in our world. There are people of different colors. Even each kernel of corn on a cob is individual and capable of recognition as such.

The more we experience diversity with pleasure and joy (rather than say, hate, prejudice or other fear-based responses), the more we become open to the truths of others and perhaps grow our own truth into something more deeply rewarding and worldly enriching. Further, through examination, we can bring our perspectives and beliefs into more realistic alignment with our personal experiences. The gift of questioning, revisiting and re-visioning in order to have experiences and truths align cohesively for us is one of the gifts we gain from our exposure to the feminine divine as presented in *The Da Vinci Code.* Those outside the academic arena of our Western culture may not have been exposed to nor experienced the feminine divine, so this book gives them a new perspective and/or new questions to ask of science, theology, philosophy and their own reality. Meanwhile, the feminine divine has been written about, recaptured and fantasized about by women, feminists, theologians in the West and the East for several decades, at the least. This article is about three of these women thinkers and their writings, and how our embodied and personal experience of the deity can, should and must include the feminine divine.

When the ideas these women and others propose become part of the popular culture through such works as the book or the movie *The Da Vinci Code*, our society can then become aware of the feminine divine, thus inspiring a more complete experience of not only the deity but also of life (simply because the feminine is included and not ignored, berated nor diminished). In short, when we are exposed to Her, we can question Her absence. When we experience Her, we bring value and ethics into our world, because we have experienced the relation between perceived opposites. As we experience diversity, such as the feminine divine offers, we experience the relations *between* things. And, it is the relations between things that move life and creation. When we experience Her, therefore, we learn that life can offer us diversity and we need not be afraid of it. We can realize that She is, alongside and in relation to any other belief, rather than in opposition.

Judith Plaskow has proven herself as a feminist and devoted Jewish theologian over some 30 years of exploration into her own religion, her own beliefs and the perspectives of her world. She has written numerous articles and several books; however, the focus of this writing shall be her first major work *Standing Again at Sinai: Judaism from a Feminist Perspective.* Certainly, one of the threshold activities of all feminist inquiry is questioning the assumptions of the established system in order to better align one's experience with the truth of diversity and relation. Plaskow does this with depth and blatant honesty. Plaskow begins her inquiry and visioning in *Standing Again* by exposing the injustice in Judaism as it relates to the exclusion of women and the feminine.

God is the one power over all of the world and It is, typically, only male. Families, political societies and cultures emulate the deity and its relation to and power over the world. The deity, thus, provides the culture with an ideal personification of shape, size, gender and behavior: "Moreover, if God is male, and we are in God's image, how can maleness *not* be the norm of Jewish humanity?" (Plaskow 8). If that is the case, and maleness is the norm, which she alleges is the case, then what about the other half of the Jewish people, as it were: what about the women? They cannot be the norm. In fact, they cannot be but supporters (and even invisible ones at that) of the males. But, simply adding women to the mix of leadership and authority and then stirring is not the solution, either. For Judaism, explains Plaskow, there must a multilayered approach. Judaism has the Law (*halachah*) and the Torah (Hebrew Bible) and Israel (nationhood) to deal with, and all of these together form the base of Jewish life. They must each be closely investigated and questioned for the stories and experiences of the women. Judaism has excluded women and made them virtually invisible. Even their invisibility has been and continues to be invisible. This attitude has amounted to an injustice and must be remedied. Jewish Feminist thought demands that women not only be included but also that the feminine divine be recognized and included, too.

The feminine divine must be incorporated into the experience of God. Using only male images, characteristics and pronouns gives only a partial picture of the deity. The complete deity is expressed as both female and male in the world. The apparent opposites are in relation to each other and this relation is what moves into and as creation. Merely interjecting female images can do little to counter the dominant male picture of so many centuries, where male images used in speaking about, to and even for God (as do the prophets) are hierarchically structured so that female is Other, less than and often invisible, while males are the normative and hierarchically superior Jews. Male-dominated hierarchies result in women being excluded from the Torah as agents of their own stories. Further, it excludes women from creating or interpreting the Law (*halachah*). Women are, as Rachel Adler (another Jewish feminist theologian) says, the peripheral Jews. "Once images become socially, politically, or morally inadequate . . . they are also religiously inadequate," declares Plaskow unequivocally (135). In other words, once women are peripheral in the community, they are also peripheral in the synagogue. Plaskow suggests, as do most feminists, that we re-image the deity in such a way as to make the human and natural symbols more fluid. The relation between the various symbols and expressions in all of life, including of the deity, is the key. The point is that when a symbol has become fixed and normative (as has the symbol of the male deity), it loses its efficacy as symbol and risks being so real it is now the only image allowed, making it blasphemous to the tradition, since use of this image is tantamount to idolatry. Symbols have their meaning through and in the relation between the symbolized and the symbol, itself. The range of experiences of the divine must be opened to allow women and men to experience the fullness (and, arguably, the reality) of the deity. If and when the feminine divine is incorporated into Jewish liturgy, recaptured in the Torah and re-visioned in the Law (*halachah*), the symbol of and for God will become appropriately relational, whole and more realistically in line with our experience of the world, where all life is in relation to itself and other life and it is in, as and through these relations that life expresses.

In feminist theology, African-American women's theological discourse is termed womanist theology. One of the leading womanist theologians is Karen Baker-Fletcher. We will look closely at the images of the feminine divine in her work *Sisters of Dust, Sisters of Spirit: Womanist Wordings on God and Creation.* In her poetic and persuasive manner, Baker-Fletcher notes that Jesus as God is God embodied in a creature on earth and therefore it is only logical to extend that reality to all creation, everywhere. God is in all creation. Theology should be embodied, should be about our experience of God and heaven, right here in our own life and body.

Baker-Fletcher argues that we need to look beyond the male and female images of God, and instead experience God as Spirit—the Spirit that lives in all of life. This approach means that life is in God. Her version of pantheism leaves the reader a bit confused but the feeling still holds: literally, all is in God; and figuratively, God is in all—both concepts together seem to form her theism—"We are within it and it is within us" (119). Spirit is fluid and everywhere present. By the end of her work, she points out her appreciation for the term "Ha Shem," which is Hebrew for "The Name." She wishes, by this reference, to indicate that God is already within all the names ever given. In fact, God is the "very source of our lives and of our power to name" (127). As with Plaskow, and most every other feminist theologian, she emphasizes that we experience God through and in our bodies. Our body is, therefore, the first place we experience and know the sacred. If we are in female bodies, then we know and experience God first in these female bodies. Again, similar to Plaskow above, she writes that if we humans are imaged in the likeness of God, and we are both male and female, then it "is possible to image God as male and female" (113). We must love what God loves and that means the diversity of our bodies and in creation. God is then the sister, the mother, the brother and the father. All of these images are used. Baker-Fletcher cites the poet Ntozake Shange who wrote that she found God in herself "and I loved her fiercely" (112).

Through these ideas and words, we can see that the feminine divine is as real and immanent for Baker-Fletcher as is the masculine divine. For her, the relation between these two aspects of the divine does not mean that one must be dominant or superior. It means, rather, that the two are as real as is the reality of the diverse bodies through and in which the divine expresses. Just as the human is both "dust" and "spirit" in relation, so is the divine both feminine and masculine in relation. All of nature expresses the relation of the seeming opposites. But, opposites are only such if they are not in relation. If they are in relation to each other, they are life itself, creating, expressing and experiencing. It is our perspective, our awareness that makes the difference. When we are aware of the feminine divine, as books and movies such as *The Da Vinci Code* encourage us to become, we come closer to seeing the world as the web of relations that is the truth of reality. We are diverse and multilayered and so are the relations of, between and in life. Such diversity expresses through the bodies and things that we know in life. Baker-Fletcher wants us to realize that the diversity of and in all nature (of which humans are a part) is the true expression of the deity.

One of the grand elders of feminist theology is Rosemary Radford Reuther. In this short writing, I will focus on only one of her many laudable works: *Sexism and God-Talk: Toward a Feminist Theology*. This work is a radical and groundbreaking critique of Christian theology. She challenges the systematic male Christian theologian about as much or more as Dan Brown in *The Da Vinci Code*.

The tradition of story-telling in Judaism that supplements the Torah is called Midrash. Many feminist scholars and writers from various religious traditions have used the tool of Midrash to bring women back into the stories of the sacred texts. In this imaginative and well-researched book, Reuther starts out with a Midrash about the death of Jesus of Nazareth. She writes that Mary Magdalene was witness to the resurrection, as she crouched for two days at the tomb. Mary then had a vision that spoke to her and she understood it to be Jesus. It told her that she would now continue the presence of the Messiah, who has gone into her future. She must not look back. Mary went to the disciples and told of the instructions given to her by the vision that was Jesus. The men would not listen. They believed that they, as men, must be in charge and that meant, among other things, having power over the women, as other. This response troubled Mary deeply and she prayed for guidance and solace. She had spoken of the peaceful and heavenly world and the disciples had berated and shunned her. Her prayer ends with: "Perhaps something of this other [Mary's own] vision will still get through the distortion [begun by Peter and continued]. Other people, even women like myself, will glimpse something of the true vision, and they will recognize me as their sister" (11).

Carefully and deeply rooted in evidence and history, Reuther takes us into the heart of an experience that any woman can imagine, where Mary's voice is the narrator/storyteller. She takes us into the heart of Mary Magdalene. Hermeneutics is the method whereby we wish to learn about the author or the one speaking. Reuther employs this useful technique to gain entry into the heart of Mary Magdalene. She then turns the information over to us through a delightful and useful Midrash. Hermeneutical investigation is a common methodology used by feminists when reaching into sacred texts, history books or even art. What did the author or artist mean? Who was that artist? Why did the artist create just that work? Since our own understanding of anything must always begin with our own experience, the deeper we experience the creative activity of an other, the better we can know the fullness of the message in and of their work. In this way, all the so-called objective sources of the various religions (and other disciplines) are really a compendium of human experiences. Also, this approach allows for feminist reconstruction of sacred story, bringing women (and our stories and lives) back into history. Historical roots and midrashic stories form the basis of Reuther's work in this book.

Reuther aptly reviews archaeological evidence that allows her to conclude, as is alluded to in *The Da Vinci Code,* that "the most common ancient human image of the divine was female" (47). In this time, people cooperated with the forces of nature, as they could not control them (as we think we can today). As the ancient peoples moved from being entirely dependent on the earth, to more agrarian lifestyles where farming and irrigation allowed some planning, the deity took on more of the attributes of the sovereign who owned or ruled the earth or some plot of it. According to Reuther, it was common, in this Near Eastern, pre-agrarian world (to which we are heir), for the mythical female deity to have power over the earthly king, who was completely dependent on Her. Gender division, however, was not a primary tool for explaining the world or the deity (-ies). Reuther postulates logically that the male monotheistic religions emerged from the more nomadic peoples of the Ancient Near East, since they did not have a relation with the earth and gardening. In those societies of more nomadic peoples, the connection to the earth was shaped by cycles, because of the life-giving and life-taking of the earth and its expressions or activities. Nonetheless, whatever the reasons, we can know today that we have inherited a patriarchal and hierarchical model from these ancient peoples, and it survives largely intact. The deity is the angry, jealous, warring and coercive one, who plays favorites, has a temper and needs to be reminded about what is really just and righteous. It remains a mystery, however, to all disciplines as to why and how we got to such an unsatisfactory and incomplete God figure from beliefs in the feminine divine as, at least, part of the deity's expression.

Even as Reuther points to this unsatisfactory conclusion, she brings out the female use of imagery in the First Testament to prove that the feminine divine was and is always present. First, she points to the Hebrew word for mercy or compassion, *rechem*. She cites Phyllis Trible (Hebrew Bible scholar of note) who points out that the root of this word is also the same root for the word "womb." Many feminists, especially Jewish feminist theologians, have begun to use this word and its derivations in place of or alongside the male images for God. Reuther also brings out the Wisdom literature of the First Testament, exposing the notion that Wisdom is feminine. Solomon, the Wise, takes Wisdom as his bride (see Hebrew Bible, Wisdom of Solomon 7:25-26, and 8:2-9). But, Reuther notes that even there Sophia/Wisdom has become "a dependent attribute or expression of the transcendent male God, rather than an autonomous, female manifestation of the divine" (57). Ultimately, Reuther concludes that female imagery for Spirit, in Christianity, was not some later derivation as the religion developed. Rather, it existed before the Second Testament was canonized and, she unequivocally states, "Greco-Roman Christianity repressed it" (59).

Reuther challenges Christian theologians by declaring emphatically that we must go beyond the idea that there is a feminine side of God, whether She is Spirit or Sophia (Wisdom) or the two together. We must, instead, question the fact "that the highest symbol of divine sovereignty still remains exclusively male" (61). Feminist theology must not accept any dualism, not even the two-gendered side of God. The deity must be rooted in being itself rather than merely in transcendence. It must be the "Shalom (Hebrew for Peace as an activity of healing in the world and in relations) of our being" (71). We must realize that the deity, whether God or Goddess, liberates us from a world of dualism. It reunites us with our bodies. It is experienced in, as and through our bodies and our relations with other bodies. There is, in fact, no adequate name for this Presence. There is only the experience of It.

Turning our attention for a moment to the other Mary in the Jesus story, we note the feminine in relation to the deity who is male, as expressed through Mary worship. In particular, Mary worship was popularized from approximately the middle of the thirteenth century to about the middle of the sixteenth century. It was during this three hundred year reign that Mary devotion was expressed in "The Books of Hours." These books were kept and studied by lay people and clergy, alike. It is believed that if anyone had one book at all, it was a copy of "The Books of Hours" even above the Christian Bible. Part of their popularity arose because of the intricate and colorful pictures in the books. The images were devotional and easily accessed for feelings and experiences of devotion, even by the illiterate of the time.

These "Books" were divided into sections. The first section was always a type of calendar that recounted religious feasts and holidays on a monthly basis. The second section was composed of simple gospel lessons similar to those that would be read aloud in church. But the heart of the "Books" contained a series of prayers called the "Hours of the Virgin." Psalms, hymns and other prose and biblical readings were set out for those who wished to devote prayer to Mary throughout the day, over an eight hour period. Part of the aim was to allow the reader to have a personal experience of the deity, Jesus and Mary, all day long. These texts began their popularity with the (male) clergy who began chanting the devotions in about the ninth century. Over the next three hundred years the devotions began to appear in the prayer books in the churches. Paintings in the "Books" would illustrate the life of Jesus, while offering prayers to and about Mary.

While Mary was never seen as divine in the same way as Jesus, her status was elevated to the one to whom many would pray, thus showing their belief in her ability to grant requests, and her status alongside Jesus and the male God-the-Father. That is, until about 1568, when Pope Pius V decreed that clergy need no longer pray to the "Office of the Blessed Virgin Mary." Just three years later, this same Pope prohibited use of the "Books" altogether, unless they were new editions, approved by the Pope himself. The practice of praying the "Office of the Virgin" and of using books of hours never recovered. Unfortunately, this act disallowed many observant Christians the opportunity to experience God or Jesus, or even Mary, for themselves, or in their own homes during the time between visiting a church.

Embodied truth was cut off. Temporarily. It/She is returning, however.

We hear over and over from the above citations that our first experience of God is best understood through, by and in our own body. The three thinkers cited and the creators of the "Books of Hours" are not the only ones who emphasize this point, and they are not necessarily representative of those who do. However, we can turn to *The Da Vinci Code* (published in 2003) and realize that movements that seek to embody the experience of the divine have existed throughout time. They are irrepressible.

To know the deity through our own body is to know that the deity is as diverse in Its expressions and experiences as we are. We know today, for instance, that there are not only two genders. We know that some people are born hermaphrodites. We also know today that some feel they are born to the wrong gender, and become another gender in the course of their lives. Whatever the gender, whatever the experience, from *The Da Vinci Code* and from these writers, we can conclude that our bodily experience provides us with the first information about what is true for us, in that moment. It is to the sources of our past, and our own experiences as understood in and as our consciousness, that we must return when we finally decide to question our beliefs and assumptions.

But, that source is not just the body nor is it just our thoughts, or our reason/mind. It is the whole self and all its oppositions, complementarities and varieties. This self includes our consciousness that is also always embodied. For this writing, consciousness is described as all our thoughts, feelings and intentions combined. Thoughts include assumptions and opinions, observations and beliefs. Feelings include imagination, intuition and physical feelings of the body. Intention includes focus and motives. These three categories relate internally within the single category and externally to the other two categories, and also to and from the body in which it resides and the world. Consciousness is always embodied in a body and in relation to that body and other bodies just as the body is relating to the categories of the consciousness. This complex web of relation makes up the existence of all that is, specifically and generally.

This concept of consciousness is a part of what I have dubbed "the Metaphysic of Pan-Relation." When there is an idea that is popularized, such as the feminine divine is popularized through society's exposure and interest in *The Da Vinci Code,* it is offered as a reality for investigation and examination. It is offered through movies, books and other media of story and ideas. In this short work, we have seen the feminine divine offered through stories, research, re-interpretation and pictures of worship. In *The Da Vinci Code* we see the feminine divine offered through a murder mystery with a theological twist. Wherever the feminine divine is offered, however, we note that it is always embodied. In *The Da Vinci Code,* it was embodied in the sexual act by the heroine's grandfather. In the "Books of Hours" it was embodied through the personal experiences of the lay people. For Judith Plaskow, the feminine divine is embodied in her own experience of Judaism. Karen Baker-Fletcher showed us the feminine divine in spirit and Spirit. And, Rosemary Radford Reuther showed the feminine divine embodied in the evidence of the history (her-story) of the Ancient Near East. But, always it is our own consciousness that forms our perspectives and holds our beliefs and that is embodied in and for us, in our own experience. Gaining our own, un-prejudged experience is what these writings offer us. This is the path, for instance, told by Dan Brown in *The Da Vinci Code* as the heroine follows her own experience into knowing differently, experiencing a different truth about herself and then expressing that truth in her own way.

If we say the truth is the same for everyone, or if we say that my religion is the one true religion, we have actually disparaged the reality of relation and the inevitability of diversity. The diversity in the expressions of the divine has been discussed and picked apart in academic, feminist, theological and philosophical studies for years. Now, finally, we have a book and movie that are both popular and accessible to the general public and that bring us the feminine divine in a palatable and interesting venue. Now, even though the public thinks of this as a new phenomenon, we can know this is another step on the journey to retrieving a complete experience of the divine. We can know that it is our consciousness of relation that changes us and the way we live. Awareness of the feminine in, of and as the divine makes the world more whole, just and diverse. This is the truth our bodies tell us. The divine is not just male. It is diverse. It is as much feminine as masculine. Diversity is in relation with diversity.

Awareness of the relation between the diversities is the transformational key.

It is the job of our intellect, consciousness and bodies to open to the reality of the diversity in the expressions of and about the deity (-ies). *The Da Vinci Code* offers progress on this road that humanity must take, or as many women writers have warned, we will perish in our patriarchal, hierarchical static dualisms. Our bodies know. It is time to listen to the diversity of them. Through movies, books, sacred texts, and religious experiences, our consciousness and our bodies are informed of the many and splendid expressions of life.

Works Cited

Adler, Rachel. *Engendering Judaism: An Inclusive Theology and Ethics.* Boston: Beacon Press, 1999.

Baker-Fletcher, Karen. *Sisters of Dust, Sisters of Spirit: Womanist Wordings on God and Creation.* Minneapolis: Augsburg Fortress Publishers, 1998.

Plaskow, Judith. *Standing Again at Sinai: Judaism from a Feminist Perspective.* San Francisco: HarperCollins, 1991.

Reuther, Rosemary Radford. *Sexism and God-Talk: Toward a Feminist Theology.* Boston: Beacon Press, 1993.

CHAPTER FIVE

THE DA VINCI CODE AND WOMEN IN THE ALCHEMIC TRADITION

ROSA MARIA STOOPS, UNIVERSITY OF MONTEVALLO

One of the most controversial theories in the book *The Da Vinci Code* is the assertion that because Mary Magdalene was not recognized by the founders of the Christian Church as the wife of Jesus, mother of His child and an apostle, the sacred feminine was forever eradicated from the Christian tradition. According to the book, the suppression of Mary Magdalene from scripture and rite by itself constitutes the reason and perpetuation of discrimination against women for two millennia, and it is time to re-evaluate the Bible, the Church, and the lies of its founders. The suppression of the sacred feminine from the Christian Church, specifically from the Catholic Church, is an extraordinarily contentious theory which is not supported by historical events or canonical documents throughout the centuries. The sacred feminine has been recognized by the Church since its inception and later with the recognition of the Virgin Mary as the queen of the Catholic Church and with the recognition of numerous female martyrs, saints, and secular members of the Church. Women were recognized by the predecessors from whom Christianity took inspiration as an important part of spiritual transformation. In ancient times, in Christ's lifetime, in the New Testament, and in modern times women have constituted an important part of the Christian tradition. During the Renaissance the recognition of the sacred feminine permeates all aspects of spiritual and artistic expression. The beatification of female martyrs and saints in the Renaissance also coincides with the sanction by the Church of the alchemic practice. The recognition of the alchemic practice would seem to be an isolated event, unrelated to the problem of the sacred feminine, if it were not for the fact that the alchemic process in the Renaissance is seen as an equivalent of the process of spiritual improvement sought by the church. In the alchemic process the female element is recognized as one half of the universe and essential for spiritual transformation.

The Da Vinci Code attempts to challenge Christianity and provoke a schism within the Church armed with audacious interpretations of newly discovered documents and a good dose of alternative history. It is precisely in suggesting a rewriting of history and scripture where author Dan Brown gets in trouble with academics, historians, and theologians.

In *The Da Vinci Code* two explosive points related to the sacred feminine are presented: The first one is that Jesus and Mary Magdalene were married, that she was pregnant with his child at the moment of the crucifixion, that she fled to France where she gave birth to a daughter that became the mother of many of the European ruling families that survive until this day, arriving to the conclusion that Mary Magdalene represents the actual Holy Grail where the seed of Christ was deposited, and that finding her remains would represent finding the most sacred object in the history of Christianity. Second, that throughout history, the Christian Church, or most specifically, the Catholic Church has followed a policy of discrimination of women that basically eradicated the sacred feminine in Christianity from its inception.

In the words of character Leigh Teabing, the reader learns that:

> The quest for the Holy Grail is literally the quest to kneel before the bones of Mary Magdalene. A journey to pray at the feet of the outcast one, the lost sacred feminine. […] A tomb containing the body of Mary Magdalene and the documents that tell the true story of her life. At its heart, the quest for the Holy Grail has always been a quest for the Magdalene—the wronged Queen, entombed with proof of her family's rightful claim to power. (257)

Experts in religion such as Drs. James L. Garlow and Dr. Peter Jones in *Cracking Da Vinci's* Code; Dr. Darrell Bock in his books *Was Jesus Married?* and *Breaking the Da Vinci Code;* Sandra Miesel and Carl Olson in *The Da Vinci Hoax: Exposing the Errors in The Da Vinci Code*; and Bart Ehrman in *Truth and Fiction in The Da Vinci Code* have dismantled several of Brown's conspiracy theories.

With regard to the marriage of Jesus Christ and Mary Magdalene, experts believe that a thorough and accurate analysis of documents used by Brown, such as the *Scrolls of Nag Hammadi* and the *dossiers secrets*, both found around the second half of twentieth century, does not substantiate claims of a marriage between Jesus Christ and Mary Magdalene, no matter how much the author attempts to stretch his interpretation of the facts contained in such documents vis-à-vis centuries of study and research by theologians and historians of the facts narrated in the New Testament. Many of the historical and religious claims of the book have been discredited by historians and theologians and at this time the speculation of a marriage between Jesus Christ and Mary Magdalene remains unproven and skepticism continues to grow; however, *The Da Vinci*

Code still leaves open a spectacular gender issue that traces its origins to religious matters. Brown explains that according to the Gospel of Philip the obliteration of the sacred feminine—by overlooking Mary Magdalene's alleged role in Christ's life— occurs from the very beginning of the Church with Peter's usurpation of the power that rightfully belonged to Mary Magdalene to be the founder of the Christian Church, given her relationship of marriage with Christ. As evidence of his theory, Brown resorts to filling gaps in the newly discovered documents with sheer speculation, for example, the passage in the *Gospel of Philip* where he says Jesus used to kiss Mary Magdalene on the mouth and call her "companion" (Miesel). The religious implications of such conjectures are enormous because they challenge the foundation not only of the Catholic Church but of all other churches that believe in the chastity, purity, and divinity of Jesus as the Son of God and have made Christ the model for spiritual perfection. Brown assures the readers that historical evidence proves that Mary Magdalene was married to a sexually active Christ and pregnant at the moment of the crucifixion.

The theoretical marriage of Christ to Mary Magdalene is not a new issue and awareness about the Priory of Sion has existed for centuries, independently of the discovery of the *dossiers secrets* that Brown claims as the triggering event for his presumptions. The Merovingian claim or the Merovingian heresy, as this theory is also known, has been around since the beginning of Christianity in France, where the Merovingians, French people of Jewish descent, became powerful rulers. The Merovingians claimed their ancestry from David and Solomon, posturing as Christians of direct descent from Jesus Christ through Mary Magdalene. In the twentieth century, the lineage of Mary Magdalene and Christ would be so broad that it would appear as if many important families of Europe were Merovingians of Jewish descent. But there is an important element that Brown does not take into account: the history of the Jewish Merovingians is also surrounded by infamy. The Merovingians did become the royalty of Europe, mainly of France, claiming their ancestry from the houses of Israel and promulgating a heretical version of the Gospel shunned by most Christians. This heretical version is the new, alternative history reintroduced by *The Da Vinci Code* in an almost word by word repetition of the Merovingian heresy.

The role of Mary Magdalene in this conspiracy theory has brought renewed interest in the book because of its potential as a modern weapon against the Roman Catholic Church, selectively aiming at the vulnerable aspect of the Church's denial to ordain women or to allow priests to marry. It is obvious in the book that a political and extreme feminist agenda is manipulated and distorted with the purpose of reviving the issue of women's equality in the Church, the ordination of women, and the right to marry for the priesthood. In chapter 74 of *The Da Vinci Code* a ritual of the Priory of Sion is described as the public sexual union—rightly referred to as *hieros gamos*—of Jacques Saunière and his wife. Robert Langdon, the novel's main character, explains that the purpose of the rite was the communion with God through sexual orgasm: "'By commuting with woman'—Langdon said—, 'man could achieve a climactic instant when his mind went totally blank and he could see God'" (309).

The Da Vinci Code attempts to cover with a spiritual varnish a rite that has no space in Christianity precisely because of the historically confirmed fact that holy men such as Jesus avoided the temptations of the flesh in order to attain a connection with God based on spiritual perfection, as Bart Ehrman states in his book *Truth and Fiction in the Da Vinci* Code: "[In the Church] all people, men and women, are to live lives of complete chastity. Those who are married are not to engage in sex; those who are unmarried should remain unmarried. By being chaste, a person can inherit the kingdom of God" (169-70). Numerous religious writings through the ages endorse chastity as a means to achieve spiritual perfection as it is corroborated in several accounts of the lives of apostles and saints. According to Katherine Gill in her article "Women and the Production of Religious Literature in the Vernacular 1300-1500," in Domenico Cavalca's book *"Lives of the Holy Fathers" (Vite dei santi padri),* which first appeared in the year 1352, there is a story specifically about chastity, and curiously it also involves Mary Magdalene:

> Citing Jerome[16] as his source, Cavalca begins his version by informing his audience that the Magdalene had been betrothed to John the Evangelist, who then jilted her on their wedding night in order to withdraw to the desert. Their wedding, he continues, was the very marriage at Cana where Jesus turned the water into wine. The Gospel writers frequently omit details like this, explains the narrator, because, as here, everyone would have known who the bride and groom were. Mary, very much in love with John, was utterly distraught after her abandonment. In dishonor she returned to confinement in her family's house, confused and stunned because "the man to whom she had given all her love had

---

[16] St. Jerome, Patron of libraries, was born Eusebius Hieronymous Sophronius,. He was the most learned of the Fathers of the Western Church. He was born about the year 342 at Stridonius. While at Rome in the time of Pope Damasus, he wrote a book on the perpetual virginity of the Virgin Mary against one Helvidius, who maintained that Mary had not remained always a virgin but had had other children by St. Joseph, after the birth of Christ. In this book Jerome made a vehement defense of virginity as a means of spiritual perfection. While at Rome he made a revision of the current Latin New Testament, and of the Psalms. Then he undertook the translation of most of the books of the Old Testament directly from the Hebrew. In the sixteenth century the great Council of Trent pronounced Jerome's Vulgate the authentic and authoritative Latin text of the Catholic Church, although the Church never implied a preference for it as superior to the original text or superior to versions in other languages. (Catholic Online)

> given himself to a love she herself did not yet understand." ("I bring this up," intervenes the narrator, "because worldly people have too much blamed Mary for the bad life she lived for a short time.")

If we take just these two sources we may speculate that John the Evangelist was aware of his calling, and inspired by Christ, shunned the temptations of the flesh in order to live a life of chastity for the highest aspiration, the communion with God. This document also serves to shed a different light on Mary Magdalene.

In order to make the Catholic Church yield to the agenda of a more permissive society that requires a "modernized" Church with female and married celebrants, Brown irresponsibly trashes the historical figure of Christ in *The Da Vinci Code*, presenting Him as a man of flesh and blood that fell to the temptations of the flesh and committed the same sins that He came to redeem, among them the original sin. Brown either lacks knowledge of doctrine or maliciously chooses to ignore the fact that since the Council of Nicea in 787 the Church has allowed the worship of the Virgin Mary, mother of Christ as model of female perfection. Some, such as Richard Wightman Fox, author of *Jesus in America* applaud the appearance of *The Da Vinci Code* and its claims by arguing that *The Da Vinci Code* "is riding the wave of revulsion against corruption in the Catholic Church [...] What Brown's novel taps into above all is a persistent American desire to recapture the true original Jesus. 'That's what Protestantism itself has always been about'" (*US News and World Report,* April 2005). Both Brown and Fox aim at exposing the Catholic Church as corrupt and attempt to "recapture" a Jesus figure that would be a more suitable model for these days, but they consistently overlook the fact that the historical Jesus emanating from documents authenticated for centuries was committed to chastity not as a result of a view of women as sinners, or of sex as sin, but rather in his desire for physical purity that transcended all human temptations to become spiritually perfect and closer to God. In Chapter 60 of *The Da Vinci Code* Leigh Teabing suggests that: "'The early church feared that if the lineage [of Christ and Mary Magdalene] were permitted to grow, the secret of Jesus and Magdalene would eventually surface and challenge the fundamental Catholic doctrine—that of a divine Messiah who did not consort with women or engage in sexual union" (257 insertion mine).

Brown continues to back his marriage theory by assuring the readers that the "true" events are depicted in the rendition of the *Last Supper*, a painting by Leonardo da Vinci, who, according to Brown was somehow aware of the truth and left a number of symbols in his painting for others to discover the truth, but even the Gnostic Gospels, which Brown cites as powerful testimony of the role of Mary Magdalene in the life of Christ, do not come close to definitely inform of an actual marriage between the two, only that they had a special relationship.

Teabing has to recognize as much: "[In the Gospel of Philip] Teabing flipped through the book and pointed out several other passages that, to Sophie's surprise, clearly suggested Magdalene and Jesus had a romantic relationship" (246).

Dan Brown speculates that among the participants of the Last Supper Mary Magdalene can be seen seated at a place of honor next to her consort, an event that conclusively attests to her identity as the Holy Grail, traditionally thought to have been the cup that Jesus used in such occasion. In the words of Sophie Neveu: " You said you have a *picture* of this woman who you claim is the Holy Grail." "Yes," answers Teabing "but it is not I who *claim* she is the Grail. Christ Himself made that claim" (242).

Through Teabing, Brown then proceeds to make an audacious interpretation of the "symbols" in the painting. Brown's interpretation is highly imaginative and his knowledge of symbols seems accurate, but he concludes as a fact that the person sitting next to Christ is a woman, a stunning affirmation not corroborated by fact. Sandra Miesel, in an interview with NBC, states that Leonardo da Vinci's own notes and sketches on this particular painting leave no doubt that the person sitting next to Jesus is actually the Apostle John. A young, beardless man with long hair, who actually fits very accurately other renditions of young men by Leonardo, should not be mistaken for a woman. Historical information shows that the twelve apostles chosen by Christ to accompany him in the last supper were all males, and Mary Magdalene was not present at that event and the symbols in the painting do not constitute a testimony of the events that took place in the real last supper.

With regard to the second assertion in *The Da Vinci Code* that the Church has traditionally discriminated against women, biblical and historical documents do not point to the Church as the instigating force behind such discrimination either. It is true that Brown considers the Bible a historically inaccurate and biased document unworthy of credibility, as Teabing asserts: "The Bible is a product of *man,* my dear. Not of God. The Bible did not fall magically from the clouds. Man created it a historical record of tumultuous times, and it has evolved through countless translations, additions, and revisions. History has never had a definitive version of the book" (231). Brown presents himself as a rigorous critic of the Bible, dismissing centuries of corroboration by historians and theologians, but chooses to give absolute credence to documents such as the *dossiers secrets*, the scrolls of *Nag Hammadi* and the *Gnostic Gospels*, all discovered in the twentieth century, the authenticity of which has not been completely established.

Brown assures his readers that early in the history of the Church the sacred feminine was forever eliminated from Christian orthodoxy, and again most specifically from Catholic doctrine, to which Brown ascribes a blatantly misogynistic view. Dan Brown and *The Da Vinci Code* advance these speculations against the Church in order to exploit the gender issue among the uninformed, taking advantage, for example, of the fact that as a mainly Protestant society, the American public does not follow the communications of the Catholic Church. The author openly exploits the issue of corruption to extend it to gender discrimination; however, in the same way that there are no definitive written records of marriage, pregnancy, and a bloodline of Christ and Mary Magdalene, there are no written records from early or contemporary Christianity that the church in fact considered women spiritually inferior. Social, economic, political, and intellectual considerations have a bigger role to play in the secular societies in which Christ was born and before the foundation of the Catholic Church. In her book *Women and Spiritual Equality in Christian Tradition*, Patricia Ranft makes an in-depth analysis of the role of women in Christian religion from the early years in order to examine the traditional claim that Christianity did have a misogynistic start. The book was published in 1998, five years before *The Da Vinci Code.* Ranft's analysis includes early Christian communities and writings, fourth century, late antiquity, the Middle Ages, Reformation, Counter Reformation, and Enlightenment periods, reaching the conclusion that from an exclusively theological point of view, the baptized woman enters a realm of freedom in which "she is in principle, freer than any other woman. The hitch, however has always come from the practical impossibility, until our own day, of implementing this freedom in a world which does not yet recognize it" (211) and continues "The early Fathers indeed endeavored to guarantee to woman the possibility of spiritual freedom [...] Whatever motivations and justification may explain the peculiar phenomenon by which the Church eventually closed doors which the Gospel and the early tradition had left open to women, the theological question is unavoidably mooted" (211-12).

Ranft does not deny that there has been discrimination against women both in society at large and in the Church through the ages and that the Church did not aggressively condemn these practices in an effort to maintain the peace with societies that considered males superior to women. Ranft attributes the discrimination of the feminine not to Christian or specifically Catholic doctrine, but to social, economic, and political considerations that persist even today. No document within the Church endorses explicit discrimination against women, although it is true that for centuries the Church does not take upon itself the vindication of women against male domination in the organization of secular society. The discrimination of women is not the result of a misogynistic position from the Catholic Church, but comes rather as a legacy of its Jewish background, where it was unthinkable to give women positions of social or ecclesiastical authority. With few exceptions pre-Christian women in Jewish societies were kept in a state of subjection which prevented their participation in any kind of government or liturgy.

According to Ranft, during the late Middle Ages and after there was a remarkable growth in the influence of women in the Church. Joan of Arc was rehabilitated in 1456 and many women achieved sainthood. In fact, there is no other Church, Christian or otherwise, where such a great number of women have been recognized for their sacrifice and elevated to martyrdom and sainthood as in the Catholic Church. There are also a great number of influential secular women who exerted great influence within the church.

The religious writings approved by the church in each particular period do not expressly encourage the type of discrimination against women that Brown would like us to believe through his premise of the suppression of the sacred feminine by the Christian Church that needs a secret society to thrive especially if such organization, in this case the Priory of Sion, advocates the denial of Christ's divinity and purity.

In the Renaissance, there was an interesting event that I would like to cite as an argument for the importance of women in the Christian tradition. In the XV century, the practice of alchemy was accepted by the Catholic Church. Alchemy, or the Great Art, often makes us evoke the figure of a sorcerer or a charlatan in a laboratory attempting the impossible enterprise of changing base metals into gold. The obscure chemical practices and language of alchemy causes skepticism and alchemy is normally cast aside at first glance. However, in the Renaissance alchemy was also understood as a highly intellectual endeavor whose main objective was the attainment of spiritual perfection through transformation. Alchemy became the metaphor for transformation for the better; the concept that even the vilest or lowest of individuals could transform themselves into better individuals—the metaphorical gold—is also the goal of Christian doctrine. The XVII century German mystic Jacob Boehme, for example, attempted to explain the transformative spirit of Christianity in alchemical terms.

In the practice of spiritual alchemy there are two elements of equal importance for the transformation and harmony of the universe: the male element and the female element. In the *Christian alchemist* by Pierre Jean Fabre, published in the eighteenth century, the sacraments and the images of the Catholic Church find an actual equivalent in the alchemic process of transformation. Numerous works of art, literature, poetry, and architecture from the period celebrate the eternal feminine and its need to enter in conjunction with the masculine half in order to obtain spiritual perfection. Hermes Trismegistus, a figure revered during the Renaissance as contemporary of Moses and Father of Alchemy, was forever immortalized in a mosaic at the main entrance of the Cathedral of Sienna. The recognition of alchemy by the

Church would seem an event completely isolated from the tradition of women in the Catholic Church, if it were not because by sanctioning the practice of alchemy, the Church was explicitly recognizing the importance of women as half of all creation and a necessary agent for the betterment of the world.

In two of the most important treatises of alchemy, the *Rosarium Philosophorum* and the *Aurora Consurgens*, the latter attributed to Saint Thomas Aquinas, the union between the male and the female counterparts is illustrated as one of the first steps to the alchemic process. A male represented by a king and a female queen are shown in the moment of their sexual union. The fact that they are represented as a queen and a king attests to the equality of their contribution. They become one and from their sacrifice a new being will be born and fly to the heights of spiritual perfection that represents the hope for a better world. The characteristics of males represent the active half of Mercurious, a supraordinate concept related to the characteristics of Sol. The female counterpart, the passive half of Mercurious, is called Luna. Sol is equated to Christ and Luna with the Virgin Mary. The *Aurora Consurgens,* a treatise on the problems of opposites in alchemy believed to have appeared even earlier than 1280, was a widely known alchemic text during the Renaissance, and it indicated that Mary mother of Christ was to be the role model for Christian women through the ages: "That death which a woman brought into the world, this day hath a woman put to flight, and the barriers of hell are broken down; for death shall have no more dominion, nor shall the gates of hell prevail against her" (69). The alchemic process corroborates the importance of the Virgin Mary in Christian Catholic doctrine and there are abundant Christian images in the alchemic language of the Renaissance in addition to the one in the *Rosarium* and the *Aurora.* Once the Virgin Mary was recognized and granted her rightful place as the mother of God, the alchemists saw this event as the final universal harmony of four elements, represented in Christian doctrine as God, the Son, the Holy Spirit, and the Virgin. Paracelsus explains that the *prima materia* in alchemy was a feminine principle containing in itself all the possibilities of life and existence. This particular language of the feminine principle was repeated almost exactly by the late Pope John Paul II. The Pope wrote numerous books on the worship of the Virgin Mary and her importance in the women's rights movement, of which he mentions:

> In our times the question of "women's rights" has taken on new significance in the broad context of the rights of the human person. *The biblical and evangelical message* sheds light on this cause, which is the object of much attention today, *by safeguarding the truth about the "unity" of the "two,"* that is to say the truth about that dignity and vocation that result from the specific diversity and personal originality of man and woman. *(Mulieris Dignitatem)*

The late Pope expressly recognized the spiritual equality of women within the Church and in society, clarifying many misconceptions and taboos, such as the accusation that the Church limits the role of women to mothers and wives. Although asserting that these roles provide spiritual satisfaction to women because of their female nature as nurturers, and considering the sacrifices that being a mother and wife entails, Pope John Paul stated that women have the right to all privileges that men enjoy, including a career outside the home and sexual satisfaction. The Catholic Church is addressing the gender issue today by providing especial attention to women and their contribution to the economy and society. Women in Catholicism are considered especial because the mother of Jesus, Mary, was a woman. His Holiness John Paul II stated his convictions as Head of the Catholic Church on the equality of women within the Church in many documents, but I would like to refer especially to two of them: the Apostolic Letter *Mulieris Dignitatem* dated August 15, 1988, given as a sermon in Rome on the same day, and the *Letter of Pope John Paul II to Women* of June 29, 1995. Many issues related to women are discussed in detail in these two official documents, including discrimination and the reasons of the refusal by the Church to ordain a female priesthood. Pope John Paul explained that the refusal of the Church to ordain women does not emanate from basic discrimination to women but rather from what he calls a diversity of roles. Mary, mother of Christ, a woman who becomes a model for all women, was given a specific role in the enormous privilege of bringing to life the earthly Jesus. Jesus was given the specific role of choosing the Apostles and according to Scripture he chose twelve males to follow His path. Jesus and the apostles represent the model for men to follow, at least within the Church.

The theory that *The Da Vinci Code* presents as fact is that, as a result of the conspiracy to suppress Mary Magdalene as the chosen bride and apostle to carry on the legacy of Christ, the traditional role of women has suffered in the Christian/Catholic church, where women are "relegated" to mothers, wives, or prostitutes, and their contribution as half of creation forever underestimated by the Church. In an effort to advance the stretched facts in his book, Mr. Brown is guilty of ignoring and minimizing the contribution of women in religion and the recognition of those contributions by the Church, as missionaries, saints and members of the church.

In conclusion, *The Da Vinci Code* should be seen for what it is, a work of fiction and an awkward attempt to utilize the Merovingian heresy as a tool with the aim of undermining the power and authority of the Catholic Church. The believers in the Merovingian heresy and the Priory of Sion have not been successful at undermining the divinity of Jesus by showing him as an unholy man with natural temptations and desires, so they resort to a different strategy, which consists in dividing the Church by insidiously exploiting a movement that has always had the potential to split the church in two: the gender issue.

Works Cited

Aurora Consurgens. A Document Attributed to Thomas Aquinas on the Problem of the Opposites in Alchemy. Ed. Marie-Louise Von Franz. Toronto: U of Toronto Press, 2000.

Bock, Darrell L. *Breaking the Da Vinci Code.* Nashville: Nelson Books, 2004.

Brown, Dan. *The Da Vinci Code*. New York: Random House, 2003.

Catholic Online. Catholic Online Saints. "St. Jerome Doctor of the Church." http://www.catholic.org/saints/saint.php?saint_id=10.

Cuneen, Sally. *Sex: Female; Religion: Catholic*. New York: Holt, Rinehart and Winston, 1968.

Ehrman, Bart D. *Truth and Fiction in The Da Vinci Code.* New York: Oxford UP, 2004.

Garlow, James L. and Peter Jones. *Cracking Da Vinci's Code*. Colorado Springs: Cook Communication Ministries. 2004.

Gill, Katherine. "Women and the Production of Religious Literature in the Vernacular 1300-1500." *Creative Women in Medieval and Early Modern Italy: A Religious and Artistic Renaissance*. Philadelphia: U of Pennsylvania Press, 1994: 64-85.

Jung, Carl Gustave. *Alchemical Studies.* New York. Princeton UP, 1967.

—. *Mysterium Coniunctionis*. R.F.C. Hulls trans. New York, Princeton UP, 1989.

Malone, Mary T. *Women in Christianity.* New York, Orbis Books, 2001.

Miesel, Sandra and Carl E. Olson. *The Da Vinci Hoax: Exposing the Errors in The Da Vinci Code.* San Francisco: Ignatius Press, 2004.

—. "Dismantling *The Da Vinci Code.*" *Crisis* (September 2003). Article reprinted with permission from the Morley Institute a non-profit education organization for Catholic Education: www.catholiceducation.org/articles/persecution/pch0058.html.

Nigg, Walter. *Warriors of God.* New York: Alfred A. Knopf, 1959.

Ranft, Patricia. *Women and Spiritual Equality in Christian Tradition.* NewYork: Saint Martin Press, 1998.

CHAPTER SIX

THE DA VINCI CODE, MEDIEVAL GRAIL STORIES, AND THE SACRED FEMININE

HARRY BROWN, DEPAUW UNIVERSITY

In his review of Ron Howard's film adaptation of *The Da Vinci Code*, Anthony Lane unleashes the greater part of his wit and acrimony not on the film but on Brown's novel, which he successively describes as "unmitigated junk," "long and laughable," a "rubble of prose," a "folly," "baloney," and, finally, a "pompous fraud." He characterizes Brown's forty million readers as "lemmings" and "suckers," who read the book, he presumes, "because everybody on the subway is doing the same." Lane suggests that Brown belongs to the class of "nervy, worrisome authors who can't stop shoving us along with jabs of information and opinion that we don't yet require." Most severely, perhaps, he concludes that Brown's "crumbling coarseness of style" reveals a lack of "command of basic, unadorned English" (76, 78).

Lane himself seems "pompous" when he sneers at common readers, and he sacrifices a measure of credibility when he admits that he "never managed to crawl past page 100" of the novel (78). Like a hasty student, he has formed his opinion before he has done the reading. But he distinguishes himself from the mass of "Da Vinci debunkers" in one important way: he confronts *The Da Vinci Code* not as a thesis but as a literary text. For many of the faithful, the novel represents a modern heresy or a libel against Catholicism. For many in the academy, on the other hand, it is merely an inflammatory potboiler that capitalizes on conspiracy theories and shallow historical revisionism. While skeptics in both camps have been beguiled by Brown's notion that "almost everything our fathers taught us about Christ is *false*" (235), few, like Lane, have stuffed their ears with wax and paused to consider the novel not for what it pleads, but for what it is. Like Lane, I propose to consider *The Da Vinci Code* as literature, but rather than taking cheap shots at Brown's style or his audience, I seek a new understanding of the novel and its extraordinary popular appeal in the context of literary history.

As Robert Langdon and Sophie Neveu seek refuge from their pursuers at the chateau of Grail expert and Knight of the realm Sir Leigh Teabing, Langdon quips, "We're on a Grail quest, Sophie. Who better to help us than a knight?" (219). What begins as a joke, however, becomes for Brown a more consistent literary model, once the meaning of Langdon and Sophie's quest is revealed in the second half of the novel, where the Grail comes to signify four things: Mary Magdalene, the wife of Jesus and the bearer of his royal bloodline; the "Sangreal" documents proving the existence of this bloodline; Sophie Neveu, the contemporary heir to the bloodline; and, more mysteriously, the "sacred feminine." In this sense, Brown represents the quest for the Grail less as the search for a physical artifact or secret information than as a quest to join spiritually with the feminine principle in hieros gamos or "sacred marriage."

Although Brown's interpretation of the Grail derives mainly from the historical conspiracy presented in Michael Baigent, Richard Leigh, and Henry Lincoln's *Holy Blood, Holy Grail* (1982), Langdon's joke also gestures to more fundamental influences in medieval Grail stories, a literary tradition that flourished in thirteenth-century Europe and continues to find expression in contemporary culture. The laser-embossed key to the deposit box containing the Priory keystone may be read as a key to Brown's novel: "Its high-tech tooling and age-old symbolism exuded an eerie fusion of the ancient and modern worlds" (145). Likewise, Brown's novel is an age-old story couched within a modern thriller, a Grail quest involving electronic surveillance networks, digital databases, and private jets flitting across Europe at the speed of sound. To what extent, then, is the idea of the Holy Grail presented in Brown's novel related to the idea of the Holy Grail presented in medieval romances? More specifically, to what extent do medieval Grail stories reveal quests for the sacred feminine, and to what extent do they reveal something else?

Medieval Grail Stories

English-speaking readers are perhaps most familiar with the Grail story from Thomas Malory's *Morte D'Arthur*, a collection of Arthurian tales printed in 1485 and borrowed mostly from earlier French sources. On the feast of Pentecost, Malory recounts, a young knight in red armor, Galahad, arrives at Camelot, a type of Holy Spirit descended on Arthur's apostles. When this audacious knight takes his place in the *Siege Perilous*, a magical seat at Arthur's table fatal to any but the best of knights, a prophecy is fulfilled and a vision of the Holy Grail, the cup of Christ carried to Britain by Joseph of Arimathea, appears at the Round Table and provides a feast for the company. The knights vow to discover the mystery of the Grail and the quest begins.

Malory follows the paths of a handful of knights, who mostly fail in their quest because they lack purity of heart. Even Arthur's two best men, Gawain and Lancelot, fall short—Gawain because he wrongly believes he can attain the Grail through martial prowess and Lancelot because he harbors a secret, adulterous love for Guinevere, Arthur's queen. Along the way, hermits and priests appear to instruct the knights on the meaning of their adventure, a spiritual quest unlike any other they have formerly undertaken.

Only three chaste knights, Galahad, Percival, and Bors—tested by temptations and an arduous spiritual ascent—reach Corbenic, the castle of the maimed Fisher King, the guardian of the Grail. The Fisher King, the knights learn, has suffered long in waiting for the prophesied Grail knight, who will cure his mysterious infirmity and release him from his sacred charge. Galahad fulfills the prophecy, healing the Fisher King with the Lance of Longinus, the legendary spear that pierced the side of Christ on the cross. Joined by nine other knights, the three partake in a type of Last Supper, in which Christ himself appears to reveal the Grail's sacred mystery and to instruct the knights to bear the relic away from the faithless realm of Britain. The three Grail knights travel to Sarras, a city in the East, where Percival and Galahad spend their remaining years in devotion to Grail. Only Bors returns to Camelot to tell the tale.

Over the course of centuries, the Grail story has been shaped by a range of cultural influences, from Celtic legends and chivalric ideals to apocryphal gospels and Cistercian theology. Each retelling retains some older elements of the story and, in turn, introduces new ones. In earlier versions of the Grail story, for example, Percival, not Galahad, is the prophesied Grail knight, who bears a familial relation to the Fisher King and, on the completion of his quest, inherits the role of Grail keeper. In even earlier analogues, the Grail is not associated with Christ at all but rather with pagan fertility rituals.

In fact, the origin of the Grail story has preoccupied medievalists for the last century. In *From Ritual to Romance* (1920), Jessie Weston draws attention to "certain curious parallels" between Grail stories and the ritual songs of the *Rig-Veda,* "the earliest literary monuments of our race" (25). Weston concludes:

> The Grail story is not *du fond en comble* the product of imagination, literary or popular. At its root lies the record, more or less distorted, of an ancient Ritual, having for its ultimate object the initiation into the secret of the sources of Life, physical and spiritual. . . . In its esoteric "Mystery" form it was freely utilized for the imparting of high spiritual teaching concerning the relation of Man to the Divine Source of his being and the possibility of a sensible union between Man and God. (203)

R. S. Loomis, on the other hand, traces the origin of the Grail story not to the remote *Rig-Veda* but to the pagan myths of Ireland and Wales. In *The Grail from Celtic Myth to Christian Symbol* (1963), he speculates that the Welsh refugees of Anglo-Saxon conquest fled to Brittany, where they cultivated the tradition of the Breton *conteurs*, the first poets of the Grail. Loomis traces a direct line of descent from the Irish sagas to the French romances, which derive "their origin and their pristine meaning" from Celtic myth:

> It is in the early literature of these Celtic lands, so long and so closely linked by cultural bonds, that we may most profitably pursue our search. . . . Patient study of this narrative material, Welsh and Irish, enables us to recognize nearly all the basic story patterns employed in the French Grail romances, and the originals of most of their chief characters. (20)

Loomis and other advocates of Celtic origin identify *The Mabinogion*, a thirteenth-century transcription of Welsh legends, as an important source. In this text, Loomis suggests, we find the "basic story patterns" of later Grail romances: a Maimed King who must be healed by his young nephew; and the four magical gifts of the *Tuatha De Danaan*, the pagan gods of Ireland. These magical artifacts, the Cauldron of Dagda, the Spear of Lugh, the Stone of Fal, and the Sword of Nuada, both Weston and Loomis argue, become the four hallowed artifacts in later Grail romances. Most significantly, the Cauldron of Dagda, or the "Cauldron of Rebirth" holds the power to return dead warriors to life. In several of these stories, King Arthur and his knights raid Ireland or some other otherworldly place in search of this vessel. In some stories, the vessel becomes associated with a woman, its regenerative power expressed as female fertility. In "Peredur, Son of Evrawg," for example, Peredur encounters a conclave of women who collect dead knights from the wilderness, bathe them in a tub of warm water, anoint them, and return them to life. The story recounts:

> Peredur rode to the court of the sons of the King of Suffering; when he arrived he saw only women, who nonetheless rose to give him a joyful welcome. As they began to talk he saw a horse approaching with a body laid across its saddle. One of the women rose and took the body from the saddle and bathed it in a tub of warm water that was near the door, and then she rubbed it with precious ointment, whereupon the man rose alive and went to Peredur, greeting him and making him welcome. Two other men came in on their saddles, and the girl revived them as she had the first. Peredur asked why this was, and they told him that in a cave there was a monster which killed them everyday. (242)

For Weston and Loomis, "Peredur" reflects a ritual celebrating seasonal renewal, an association of the feminine principle with the cyclical fertility of nature. In this sense, scholars lend some support to Brown's interpretation of the Grail as a symbol of the sacred feminine.

More recently, however, Richard Barber has challenged scholars who seek the origin of the Grail story in antiquity or even in prehistory. In *The Holy*

Grail: Imagination and Belief (2004), Barber claims that his predecessors have substituted speculation for legitimate evidence. He argues that Loomis's "zeal for Celtic origins outran the material on which he was working, and his arguments rely on a series of assumptions and analogues which scarcely hang together." Likewise, he suggests that Weston's interpretation of the Grail as a symbol of female fertility "has haunted twentieth-century literature to a degree quite disproportionate to its basis in fact" (245, 248). Barber approaches question of origin more soberly, beginning not with undocumented rituals and myths but with the textual certainties of romances composed in France and Germany between 1190 and 1240. Although he supports Loomis's notion of a Celtic literary inheritance in medieval Normandy, he hesitates to draw broader conclusions without documentation of these connections.

For Barber, the Grail story begins with Chrétien de Troyes, the poet who formally introduced Arthurian legends to continental literature. In Chrétien's *Story of the Grail*, begun in 1188 but left unfinished by the time of his death sometime before 1190, Percival, a virtuous but ignorant knight, discovers the castle of the Fisher King, who suffers from a mysterious wound to the thighs. The king's injury signifies impotence and infertility; Chrétien, borrowing from Welsh sources, describes the kingdom of the Maimed King as a wasteland. During the course of his supper with the Fisher King, Percival witnesses a procession of four mysterious relics, also evocative of "Peredur": a broken sword, a bleeding lance, a platter, and, finally a cup. Percival fails the test, however, when he fails to ask the crucial question: "Whom does the Grail serve?" The next morning, he finds the castle abandoned. Had he inquired about the king's injury and the mysterious relics, a wandering maiden tells him, the king would have been healed and the wasteland returned to life. In his despair, Percival loses his faith in God and vows to return to the castle and heal the king. The first of the Grail romances ends here, incomplete.

Chrétien's unfinished story has proven inscrutable for generations of scholars frustrated that the poet did not live to explain the meaning of the Fisher King, the bleeding lance, or the Grail. According to scholars such as Weston and Loomis, the answer lies in Chrétien's adaptation of Celtic stories: an impotent king who rules over a dead land and the four mythical treasures of the *Tuatha De Danaan*, including a cup that contains the power to restore life. Chrétien makes no association between the Grail and Christ, nor does he connect the Fisher King to Joseph of Arimathea, the uncle of Jesus who, in later romances, brings the Grail from Jerusalem to Britain and fathers the line of Grail keepers.

In the decade following Chrétien's death, several poets resolved to finish the *Story of the Grail*, and in doing so they Christianized what had been a patchwork of pagan legend and chivalric romance. Sometime in the first decade of the thirteenth century, for example, Robert de Boron drew from the apocryphal but widely circulated Gospel of Nicodemus and forged the first connection between the Cauldron of Rebirth and the cup of Christ. In *Joseph of Arimathea*, Robert further introduces the idea that Joseph brings the relic to Britain, where he converts the pagan clans and establishes a lineage of Grail keepers. The Grail becomes the Holy Grail.

Barber identifies Robert de Boron as a crucial figure in the development of the Grail story, one who "imagines the subject in a totally different way" (40). While Chrétien might have drawn from Celtic myth, Robert establishes an historical context: "he takes the story back to the time of Christ, relating the history of the Grail to the Gospel narrative" (Barber 40). In these later French romances, Percival fulfills his promise to return to the Fisher King, where he discovers that he is part of the holy lineage, and that he is destined to replace his long lost uncle as Grail keeper. He also learns the truth of the relics that he only glimpsed earlier: the bleeding lance is the Lance of Longinus, the spear that pierced Christ's side as he hung on the cross, and the weapon that originally maimed his uncle; the cup, of course, is the cup of Christ, the vessel that held Jesus' blood at the Last Supper and the crucifixion.

This transformation of the treasures of the *Tuatha De Danaan* into Christian relics represents a significant example of the process of cultural adaptation that informs Weston's and Loomis's readings of Grail stories, and that Brown describes in *The Da Vinci Code*. As he reveals the Grail story to Sophie, Langdon illustrates the process of "transmogrification":

> The vestiges of pagan religion in Christian symbology are undeniable. Egyptian sun disks became the halos of Catholic saints. Pictograms of Isis nursing her miraculously conceived son Horus became the blueprint for our modern images of the Virgin Mary nursing Baby Jesus. And virtually all the elements of the Catholic ritual—the miter, the altar, the doxology, the communion, the act of "God-eating"—were taken directly from earlier pagan mystery religions. (232)

Even more interesting for conspiracy theorists like Baigent, Leigh, and Lincoln, however, the anonymous *Perlesvaus* and Wolfram Von Eschenbach's *Parzival*, both composed during the first two decades of the thirteenth century, associate the Grail keepers with the Templars, both by the emblem of the red cross and, in Wolfram's text, by name. While *Parzival* develops an esoteric Christian symbolism, the romance seems to retain elements of the original pagan stories of regeneration. Wolfram describes the Grail not simply as a cup, but also as a magical stone with the power to make old men young again and return the dead to life, much like the cauldron described in the *Mabinogion*:

> It is called "Lapsit exillis." By the virtue of this stone the Phoenix is burned to ashes, in which he is reborn. . . . Further: however ill a mortal may be, from the day on which he sees the Stone, he cannot die for that week, nor does he lose his color. For if anyone, maid or man, were to look at the Gral for two hundred years, you would have to admit that his color was as fresh as in his early prime. . . . Such powers does the Stone confer on mortal men that their flesh and bones are soon made young again. (239)

The Arthurian romances compiled between 1220 and 1240, which scholars call the *Vulgate Cycle* or the *Prose Lancelot*, present a collection of stories about Arthur's most famous knight, including *The Quest of the Holy Grail*. The fusion of chivalric romance with newly Christianized Grail stories, however, proved awkward, since the Grail story in the *Vulgate Cycle* is thought to have been composed by Cistercian monks hostile to the aristocratic ideals of martial valor and courtly love. These romances portray the sternest critiques of these ideals in the failure of Arthur's two greatest knights, Gawain and Lancelot. A hermit castigates Gawain for his former achievements in battle, "Do not imagine . . . that these adventures now afoot consist in the murder of men or the slaying of knights; they are of a spiritual order, higher in every way and much more worth" (*Quest* 174). And Lancelot, the paragon of courtly love, confesses his sin of adultery and disavows courtly love itself, the defining ideal of Arthurian romance:

> I have sinned unto death with my lady, she whom I have loved all my life, Queen Guinevere, the wife of King Arthur. . . . For her love alone I accomplished the exploits with which the whole world rings. She it is who raised me from poverty to riches and from hardship to the sum of earthly bliss. But I know full well that this bond is the sin that has earned me Our Lord's dire wrath. (*Quest* 89)

In the *Vulgate Cycle*, the knights who attain the Grail are distinguished from those who do not only by their chastity. Percival, a virgin in this story, receives counsel from his aunt that contains the essential message of the Cistercian Grail story:

> Sweet nephew, it so happens that you have kept so close a watch upon yourself till now that your virginity was never once abused nor smirched, nor have you ever known in verity the nature of the flesh or carnal union. And this was most essential for your good; for had your body been violated by the corruption of sin, you would have forfeited your primacy among the companions of the Quest, even as Lancelot of the Lake, who through the lusts and fevers of the flesh let slip long since the prospect of attaining what all the rest now strive after. Therefore I implore you to keep your body as undefiled as the day Our

> Lord made you a knight, so that you may come pure and unsullied before the Holy Grail, and without the stain of lechery. (*Quest* 102)

As they strive for the Grail, Percival and Bors are tempted by demons in the shape of women, who attempt to lure them from virtue first with promises of carnal pleasure and then with threats. Bors, perhaps the least worthy of the three Grail knights, endures the most difficult trials, having to sacrifice his brother's life to protect a maiden's virginity, and, later, to witness the mass suicide of a noble lady and her retainers, who throw themselves from a tower when Bors refuses to break his vow of chastity with them. As they prepare to plummet to their deaths, Bors recognizes that "He preferred them all to lose their souls rather than he his" (*Quest* 194).

Such a story that values chastity above life itself seemed to demand the creation of an entirely new figure in the tradition of Grail stories, the saintly Galahad, whose arrival at Camelot in red armor on Pentecost Sunday parallels the descent of the Holy Spirit on Christ's disciples. In other ways, Galahad parallels Christ. His name derives from Gilead, a symbolic denotation for Christ in the Old Testament. He fulfills a messianic prophecy by occupying the *Siege Perilous*, has the power to banish demons and heal the sick, and does not seem to feel the "lusts and fevers of the flesh" that torment even Percival and Bors: a great source of mockery in the film *Monty Python's Quest for the Holy Grail*, in which the childlike Galahad remains oblivious to the seductions of a gaggle of virgins.

Upon his attainment of the Grail, Galahad communes directly with Christ and, like Christ, is transfigured by the mystical experience: "Galahad drew near and looked into the Holy Vessel. He had but glanced within when a violent trembling seized his mortal flesh at the contemplation of the spiritual mysteries" (*Quest* 283). Through his status as the maternal grandson of the Fisher King, Galahad is not only the heir of Grail family, as Percival is in prior romances, but he is even more closely attached to Christ's family through his association with King Solomon, the builder of the Temple. In a later chapter of the Cistercian Grail story, the author interpolates a story into the Old Testament, in which Solomon has a vision that his line will be redeemed through Galahad. Solomon then crafts a sword and a belt from the treasures of the Temple and sets them adrift in a Miraculous Ship, which Galahad, in his own time, discovers. Girded with the sword of David, Galahad becomes a powerful emblem of the House of David.

The Da Vinci Code as Grail Quest

In *The Da Vinci Code* Langdon explains to Sophie:

> The Grail . . . is symbolic of the lost goddess. When Christianity came along, the old pagan religions did not die easily. Legends of chivalric quests for the lost Grail were in fact stories of forbidden quests for the lost sacred feminine. Knights who claimed to be "searching for the chalice" were speaking in code as a way to protect themselves from a Church that had subjugated women, banished the Goddess, burned nonbelievers, and forbidden the pagan reverence for the sacred feminine. (238-39)

To what extent, then, are medieval Grail stories quests for the sacred feminine, in the sense that Brown describes them in *The Da Vinci Code*? Certainly, in the *Vulgate Cycle*, the more recent and well-known of medieval Grail stories, the grave emphasis on chastity, on the corruption of the flesh, and on the literal demonization of women seems incompatible with the *hieros gamos* ritually enacted by Jacques Saunière and his wife Marie Chauvel in the basement of their country house. In fact, it seems to exemplify the argument presented in *The Da Vinci Code* that agents of Christian culture, like the Cistercian brothers, systematically eradicated all traces of the sacred feminine from these ancient stories.

But even the *Vulgate Cycle* betrays signs of the sacred feminine, either inherited from earlier Grail stories or original to itself. Although he shuns carnal love, Galahad encounters women at crucial moments in his quest: a woman announces the arrival of Galahad at Camelot; a woman, Percival's sister, girds Galahad with the sword of King David and confers on him his royal rank; and the same woman accompanies him with the Grail to the East and is buried by his side, joined to him in spirit if not in body. Curiously, Gawain fails in his Grail quest on July 22, the feast of Mary Magdalene, one of the few specific dates mentioned in the story, as if the "dethroned queen" herself authoritatively stifles Gawain, the emblem of the male warrior ideal.

Still, the clearest signs of the sacred feminine appear in earlier Grail stories, in Chrétien's chivalric romances and in the myths of Ireland and Wales. In Chrétien's story, Percival strives for the Grail not in spite of his amorous desires but rather to honor Blancheflor, his feminine ideal. In the *Vulgate Cycle*, two sexless angels bear the Grail into the knights' midst; in Chrétien's story, a woman bears it. This image of a woman carrying the sacred cup, if we allow Loomis's speculation, follows the earliest analogue of the Grail story: the Cauldron of Rebirth brought to humanity by Danu, the lost mother goddess of northwestern Europe, to transform death into life.

Brown proposes to do the same thing to medieval Grail stories that the Grail stories did to these earlier pagan myths. He has "transmogrified" them, retaining certain elements and neglecting others. Brown seems to mold Langdon as a Grail knight. Occasionally though never powerfully tempted by Sophie's feminine charms, he never gives in to temptation until a chaste kiss at the novel's close. Like the innocents Percival and Galahad, he wears a Mickey Mouse wristwatch as a "reminder to stay young at heart" (146-47), a signal of his own childlike virtue. The riddles he solves, like the trials faced by the Grail knights, serve to prove his worthiness, "tests of merit," as Sophie describes them (205). When Langdon finally discovers the Grail's final resting place, he expresses piety appropriate to a Grail knight who has completed his quest: "With a sudden upwelling of reverence, Robert Langdon fell to his knees" (454).

In Sir Leigh Teabing, the wealthy Grail expert maimed by polio, Brown provides a Fisher King, a repository of knowledge overburdened by his responsibility but revived by the arrival of Robert, the Grail knight, at his castle. As he tells Langdon, "I've waited my entire life to be involved" (283). In his dual role as "The Teacher" Teabing also represents a failed knight, one like Gawain and Lancelot who prove themselves unworthy of the Grail. As Teabing is dragged away by British police, Langdon gravely tells him, "Only the worthy find the Grail, Leigh. You taught me that" (426). In this respect, Teabing joins the company of failed knights: Silas, Aringarosa, Rémy, and the Papal secretary.

At the same time, Brown rejects significant elements of traditional Grail stories or offers drastic revisions. No previous story, for instance, envisions the Holy Grail manifested in a human being. As a living personification of the Grail, Sophie Neveu represents Brown's most radical revision of the Grail tradition. The end of the novel reveals that she is a hereditary descendant of Jesus and the bearer of the royal blood; she is the incarnation of the sacred feminine. But she is also quite human; she works for French intelligence, talks on a cell phone, and drives a Smart Car. In the same way that Brown fuses the ancient and the modern in his Grail story, Sophie represents a convergence of the ideal and the real, or, to use Weston's interpretation of the symbolic meaning of the Grail, a "sensible union between Man and God." Langdon's first impression of her emphasizes both the ethereal and the earthy:

> She was moving down the corridor toward them with long, fluid strides . . . a haunting certainty to her gait. Dressed casually in a knee-length, cream-colored Irish sweater over black leggings, she was attractive and looked to be about thirty. Her thick burgundy hair fell unstyled to her shoulders, framing the warmth of her face. Unlike the waifish, cookie-cutter blondes that adorned Harvard dorm room walls, this woman was healthy with an unembellished beauty and genuineness that radiated a striking personal confidence. (50)

Although it is amusing to think that Sophie's Irish sweater represents Brown's subtle gesture to the Celtic origins of the Grail legend, much as "Teabing" (an anagram of "Baigent") is a salute to his more immediate influence, Brown, nonetheless, seems to neglect the cultural origins of the Grail story described by recent scholarship. The novel asserts that the idea of the Grail originated in the Holy Land, in the years following Christ's crucifixion, when Mary Magdalene came to Gaul with Jesus's child. In fact, the *Mabinogion* and other sources suggest that the Grail story probably originated in northwestern Europe centuries before the birth of Christ. Only much later, Chrétien and others recast these myths as Christian allegory.

Still, Brown's loose interpretation of medieval Grail stories does not necessarily contradict his provocative claims about the cultural suppression of the sacred feminine and the consequent resurfacing of the sacred feminine in art and literature. Weston, in fact, offers a similar view in her survey of the transformation of pagan celebrations of rebirth into "dogmatic Medievalism, with its crassly materialistic view of the Eucharist; its insistence on the saving grace of asceticism and celibacy; and its scarcely veiled contempt for women," all of which, Weston concludes, "overwhelmed the original conception" of the Grail as a symbol of the sacred feminine (207).

Nevertheless, the interpretation of history presented in *The Da Vinci Code* and perhaps sustained by speculative readings of medieval Grail stories remains, as Barber emphasizes, impossible to prove. Like the religious ideology it proposes to subvert, it must be taken as a matter of faith that Jesus had a wife and a child; that somewhere a secret society holds the proof of this; and that, after two millennia of secrecy, the world is ready for this knowledge. At the end of the novel, Marie Chauvel tells Langdon, "The pendulum is swinging. We are starting to sense the dangers of our history . . . and of our destructive paths. We are beginning to sense the need to restore the sacred feminine" (444).

Barber remains dubious of any reading that would draw medieval Grail stories into connection with more ancient notions of the sacred feminine, let alone the conspiracy theories underlying *The Da Vinci Code*. For modern readers, he suggests, "the Grail becomes a mirror, reflecting the preoccupations of the individual writer and their intellectual milieu. . . . Nothing is taken as defined; everything in the old stories is questioned and reshaped according to the mood of the moment" (290). While Weston sees the changeability of the Grail story as evidence of its vitality, Barber worries that revisionism threatens to undermine an informed understanding of medieval literature by substituting fantasy or ideology for scholarship. He scorns the "conspiracy theory of history" and dismisses *Holy Blood, Holy Grail* "an ingeniously constructed series of suppositions combined with forced readings of such tangible facts as are offered" (310).

He would likely say the same for *The Da Vinci Code*. Although his words are more judicious than Lane's, Barber also seems to hold in contempt the mass of common readers who devour conspiracies and mistake them for revelation: "While our medieval forebears reached for the spiritual and the intangible, our materialistic age reaches only for the top shelf of the supermarket" (369).

I do not agree with Lane that the millions of readers of *The Da Vinci Code* are mindless lemmings, nor do I agree with Barber that they have been spiritually anaesthetized by consumer culture. The phenomenon of the novel, in fact, suggests that the opposite is true. Brown's novel seems to serve a similar purpose for modern readers that Grail romances served for medieval readers. Both audiences, contrary to Barber's view, seek revelation. But I also hesitate to conclude that readers find this revelation in the most obvious of the novel's claims. *The Da Vinci Code*, after all, is only one of many works of fiction and scholarship during the last three decades to radically reconsider the role of women in religious history, and I think that most who read this novel are content to leave Christianity as it is.

What intrigues so many, I think, is not the promise of a long overdue return to goddess worship and celestial orgasms, but rather the more fundamental semiotic promise of codes and clues, of the interconnectedness of knowledge, of hidden meaning, and of definite answers buried somewhere, in some secret vault. It doesn't matter that we won't ever find them. Though he never lays his hands on the Sangreal documents or the bones of Mary Magdalene, Robert Langdon still falls to his knees in pious rapture when he becomes certain, finally, that they exist in a physically definable place.

In a reflexive moment, *The Da Vinci Code* provides one of the most significant clues to its own popularity:

> As someone who had spent his life exploring the hidden interconnectivity of disparate emblems and ideologies, Langdon viewed the world as a web of profoundly intertwined histories and events. *The connections may be invisible,* he often preached to his symbology classes at Harvard, *but they are always there, buried just beneath the surface.*" (15-16)

The novel represents less a quest for the sacred feminine than a quest for this "interconnectivity." While medieval Grail stories reflected a quest for the ineffable, *The Da Vinci Code* reflects a quest for the explicable, which in this age of disparate and chaotic information has become the postmodern Holy Grail.

Works Cited

Barber, Richard. *The Holy Grail: Imagination and Belief.* Cambridge: Harvard UP: 2004.

Brown, Dan. *The Da Vinci Code.* New York: Random House, 2003.

Chrétien de Troyes. *Arthurian Romances.* Trans. William W. Kibler and Carleton W. Carroll. New York: Penguin, 1991.

Lane, Anthony. "Heaven Can Wait." *New Yorker*. 25 May 2006: 76-78.

Loomis, R. S. *The Grail from Celtic Myth to Christian Symbol.* New York: Columbia UP, 1963.

The Mabinogion. Trans. Jeffrey Gantz. Penguin: New York, 1976.

The Quest of the Holy Grail [Vulgate Cycle]. Trans. P. M. Matarasso. New York: Penguin, 1969.

Weston, Jessie. *From Ritual to Romance.* 1920. Garden City, New York: Doubleday, 1957.

Wolfram Von Eschenbach. *Parzival.* Trans. A. T. Hatto. New York: Penguin, 1980.

CHAPTER SEVEN

THE NOT SO SACRED FEMININE: FEMALE REPRESENTATION AND GENERIC CONSTRAINTS IN *THE DA VINCI CODE*

JENNIFER BRANDT, BOWLING GREEN STATE UNIVERSITY

Transcending the traditional status typically ascribed to genre fiction, the mystery and suspense elements of Dan Brown's *The Da Vinci Code* have been widely heralded by most popular press critics. The academic scholarship surrounding the novel has done little to question the text's formulaic plot and characterizations, tending to focus more on the validity of the novel's historical and artistic claims. While some scholarly attention has been granted to the role of the sacred feminine in the text, what is of particular interest to me is that there has yet to be any substantial work done looking at the role of *actual* female representation in *The Da Vinci Code*. In view of the text's overall concern with the sacred feminine and the role of women in society as a whole, this absence is a gross academic oversight. Although *The Da Vinci Code* offers a radical view of history that argues for the equality and power of women, at the end of the novel nothing has actually changed. Therefore, in this essay, I will be offering a gendered analysis of the female protagonist, Sophie Neveu. Considering that *The Da Vinci Code* is first, and foremost, a mystery/detective hybrid, the text's lack of female empowerment is ultimately a result of its generic constraints.

The Da Vinci Code begins with the murder of museum curator Jacques Saunière. As Grand Master of a secret society known as the Priory of Sion, Saunière had been in charge of guarding the location and secret of the Holy Grail. Before his death, Saunière leaves clues to the location of the Grail, and the story revolves around Harvard symbologist Robert Langdon and DCPJ cryptologist Sophie Neveu's search for the artifact. Complicating matters is the fact that Langdon is the prime suspect for Saunière's murder, and Sophie is Saunière's estranged granddaughter. As the text unfolds, it becomes apparent that the Grail is not the chalice from which Jesus drank at the last supper, but the bones of Mary Magdalene, wife of Jesus and mother of his daughter. More importantly, the Grail is a symbolic representation of the sacred feminine, which in the text represents a balance of power between men and women, an equality of the sexes.

In order to see how *The Da Vinci Code* is tied to the conventions of its genre, it is first important to establish some of the conventions of mystery and detective fiction, concentrating on the role of the detective, authority, agency, and objectification and the gaze. Focusing on the character of Sophie, I will specifically address these conventions in relation to gender, revealing how *The Da Vinci Code* is adept at questioning conventions and stereotypes, without ever really being transgressive.

Traditionally, crime narratives have revolved around male investigators. In her article "Murder, Mass Culture, and the Feminine: A View From the *4.50 From Paddington*," Angela Devas attributes this convention to the fact that,

> A detective novel concerns elements that can be seen as related to the masculine sphere, such as rationality and authority, with the detective responsible for the restoration of justice and the imposition of moral order. The persona of the detective embodies the ability to enact these qualities, and therefore the obvious candidate for this kind of role is a man. (258)

Here Devas touches upon many of the conventional characteristics ascribed to males in the genre. They are associated with rationality, authority, justice and morality, suggesting, then, that women are associated with the converse of these characteristics: irrationality; powerlessness; injustice; and immorality. Historically, in the detective genre, this is how women are viewed. Indeed, "when she does appear in the traditional story, the woman shows up as a *body* – if not the victim, then the seductress or suspect" (Mizejewski 14). As a body, women are more often than not seen as the object, rather than the subject, in these texts.

This objectification of women, then, becomes problematic, or unnatural, if she is to be seen in the active role: "Where the detective is a woman, there is therefore a disturbance in the 'natural' state of affairs and the boundaries of the genre itself are called into question" (Devas 258). Or, the classic archetype is called upon, where "a Miss Marple or a Jessica Fletcher generally operates within the domestic sphere, solving drawing-room crimes and reestablishing harmony through a combination of skillful listening, good sense, and intuitive judgment about character" (Shuker-Haines 71). A clear division is shown as to what traits are feminine versus those that are masculine. Early female detectives were differentiated from their male counterparts by being tied to the home, using domestic knowledge and good sense, as opposed to the professional training and rational fact employed by their male foils. Contrasting the archetype of the sexualized femme fatales, they were often older and matronly (like the aforementioned Miss Marple or Jessica Fletcher) further associating them to the traditional sphere of domesticity by a lack of overt and physical sexuality.

These stereotypes would change, though, in large part due to the passing of Title VII of the Civil Rights Act in 1972, which prohibited discrimination in public law enforcement hiring (Mizejewski 59). As a result of the changes this law brought about, detective and crime fiction was forced to evolve to allow women more "legitimate" roles of agency and power, resulting in the genre's establishment of new conventions pertaining to the portrayal of females. In an attempt to stay within the traditional boundaries of the genre, the female detective is often depicted under patriarchal control, be it by the constraints of judicial authority and/or a male boss, or through the professional partnering with a man. Additionally, her femininity is kept in check by placing her within the confines of Western standards of feminine beauty. The female detective's power must always be held in a series of checks and balances between masculine agency and feminine constraints. This tactic is employed in *The Da Vinci Code*, where a balance is created with the partnering of Sophie, a cryptologist working for the French judicial police, and Harvard symbologist Robert Langdon.

Interestingly, the idea of balance is central to the plot of *The Da Vinci Code*. In many ways, the protagonists' search for the Holy Grail is a search for balance. As Langdon explains in the text, "The ancients envisioned their world in two halves–masculine and feminine. Their gods and goddesses worked to keep a balance of power. Yin and yang. When male and female balanced, there was harmony in the world. When they were unbalanced, there was chaos" (Brown 36). Here, the idea of balance suggests harmony, rather than control. Throughout the text, there appears to be a balance between Langdon and Sophie as they work off their individual strengths to solve the mystery. However, upon examining the plot more closely, it becomes apparent that as the text progresses, Langdon's strengths increase as Sophie's decrease.

In her book, *Hardboiled and High Heeled: The Woman Detective in Popular Culture*, Linda Mizejewski writes, "Popular genres are gold mines for cultural studies because they tap into our fantasies and assumptions about gender, power, and sexuality. A genre like the crime story works only as long as there are readers and audiences literally willing to buy into it" (15). In general, audiences are "willing to buy into it" because although detective fiction plays with taboo subjects, the moral order is only temporarily disrupted. Typically at the end, the male detective solves the mystery, and the female, whether she is suspect, victim, or sidekick, has in some way been contained. Therefore, if *The Da Vinci Code* is going to make claims for female religious and sexual power and equality, then it can only do so under the heavy constraints of the detective formula. Audiences will not swallow such a fantastic generic invention, unless it comes with a heavy dose of conventional sexism.

Like most good mysteries, *The Da Vinci Code* begins with a murder. Museum curator Jacques Saunière has been shot in the stomach at the Louvre. By the time he is found by the police,

> He had stripped off every shred of clothing, placed it neatly on the floor, and laid down on his back in the center of the wide corridor, perfectly aligned with the long axis of the room. His arms and legs were sprawled outward in a wide spread eagle, like those of a child making a snow angel . . . or, perhaps more appropriately, like a man being drawn and quartered by some invisible force [. . .] employing his own naked abdomen as a canvas, Saunière had drawn a simple symbol on his flesh–five straight lines that intersected to form a five-pointed star. *The pentacle.* (35)

In setting up the corpse, and his plot, in this way, Brown is tapping into the very fantasies of gender and power that Mizejewski describes. Saunière is sexualized by his nudity and feminized by the goddess symbol of the pentacle. The role of the body is an important one. As Mizejewski notes,

> The detective story is all about bodies, usually beginning with homicide, the disturbing discovery of the body, a threat to meaning and order. The goal is to restore order through the justice system. But the usual machineries of justice–investigators, police, the legal system–are overwhelmingly filled with masculine, white, heterosexual bodies–an old-boys network, shot through with suspicion of women. (14)

Certainly, the spectacle of Saunière's body is a threat to meaning and order. In arranging himself in such a manner he problematizes his own crime scene, defacing himself with symbols and codes. Lead inspector Captain Bezu Fache, who is immediately identified with both the law and religious righteousness, is necessary in the text to provide balance and to be the driving force in restoring the moral order. Langdon, as the crime's prime suspect, and Sophie, as a female investigator, serve as foils to Fache's authority.

The character of Sophie Neveu serves multiple purposes within the text, and she is the main focus of my analysis of *The Da Vinci Code*. Although Langdon is positioned as the hero of the story, the mystery surrounding the death of Sophie's grandfather, and the subsequent search for the Holy Grail and the secret of Sophie's heritage, is the crux of the novel. Rather than include Sophie as a mere relative of the victim, Brown chose to portray her as an investigative cryptologist for the French police. Her career makes her slightly unnatural, yet provides her with the authority necessary for her to partner with Langdon. A codebreaker, "Sophie made her living extracting meaning from seemingly senseless data" (Brown 78). Working in a masculine specialty, she is employed making sense from chaos, a field which aligns her with meaning and order. Investigating the murder of her grandfather, she is cold and detached throughout much of the investigation, having cut herself off from him, her only family, years before. However, her need to know her family's history drives her investigation and the search for the Holy Grail. Therefore, Sophie is a character of contradictions. Although these contradictions initially work to position her as a powerful female character, ultimately her power does little else than advance the plot, and as the novel ends, the majority of the empowerment has disappeared.

The contradictions of Sophie are established with her first appearance in the text. Upon hearing that she is at the crime scene, Captain Fache thinks,

> Sophie Neveu was one of the DCPJ's biggest mistakes. A young Parisian *déchiffreuse* who had studied cryptology in England at the Royal Holloway, Sophie Neveu had been foisted on Fache two years ago as part of the ministry's attempt to incorporate more women into the police force. The ministry's ongoing foray into political correctness, Fache argued, was weakening the department. Women not only lacked the physicality necessary for police work, but their mere presence posed a dangerous distraction to the men in the field. As Fache had feared, Sophie Neveu was proving far more distracting than most. (Brown 49-50)

This description is the reader's first introduction to the character. Although she is part of the police force, her authority is immediately questioned by Fache's assertion that she is there as a result of "political correctness." Further, she and her female contemporaries are weaknesses due to their physicality, a physicality that instead of embodying strength, works as a type of distraction. She is not characterized as an active body, but rather, as an objectified one. And, fitting in with historic generic conventions, she is a body that is dangerous.

Langdon's description adds to her objectification. He describes Sophie as,

> Dressed casually in a knee-length, cream-colored Irish sweater over black leggings, she was attractive and looked to be about thirty. Her thick burgundy hair fell unstyled to her shoulders, framing the warmth of her face. Unlike the waifish, cookie-cutter blondes that adorned Harvard dorm room walls, this woman was healthy with an unembellished beauty and genuineness that radiated a striking personal confidence. (Brown 50)

By comparing Sophie to "waifish, cookie-cutter blondes" he is associating her with something other than typical female representations of female beauty. At the same time, though, he is confirming her "to-be-looked-at-ness" by concentrating on her physical appearance, suggesting her confidence comes from her "unembellished beauty."

In looking at these descriptions, the context in which they are given must be taken in account. In *Busybodies, Meddlers, and Snoops: The Female Hero in Contemporary Women's Mysteries*, Kimberly Dilley writes, "The norms and expectations of genre fiction are enmeshed with the norms and expectations of society. Focusing on genre fiction exposes how gender enters into, and is constructed by, the form" (Dilley 59). With this precept in mind, Fache's comments can be seen to reflect the unease that Mizejewski discusses when she writes, "Police departments and federal agencies were radically jolted by these laws [Title VII], which literally demanded reimagining the *bodies* on the force" (59). Throughout most of the text, Fache is an unlikable character. However, it would be remiss to merely dismiss his remarks due to his initial characterization. First of all, Fache is a character associated with authority, which therefore lends credibility to his comments. Secondly, by the end of the novel, Fache is seen in a much softer light, and his initial distastefulness is redeemed. Most importantly, though, is what Dilley and Mizejewski suggest, that Fache and Langdon's comments are more than just that of characters, but rather, they are a reflection of real-life, societal beliefs.

As for Langdon's comments, in many ways they are necessary to the text in providing the reader with a mental picture of the character. However, in his comparison of her to other women, and linking her confidence with her attractiveness, Langdon's description aids in the objectification of Sophie. Further, Fache and Langdon's descriptions are given before the reader has any actual contact with the character, giving these two male characters authority over her. It is through their lens that the reader begins to view Sophie. Even though she takes an active role in the scenes immediately following the descriptions, she is first, and foremost, seen by the readers as a body, not a mind.

Immediately following these descriptions, Sophie is in her most powerful position in the text. Interestingly, though, it is a power based on deceit. She lies to get access to the crime scene, she lies to Fache and Langdon regarding her purpose there, and she abets Langdon's escape from the Louvre. Here Sophie is working most definitely outside of the law. In looking at the role of the female detective, Dilley writes,

> As an officer of the state, the woman "police-trained" detective joins a predominantly male profession. She must work in company with these men on a daily basis. The woman is granted a degree of authority and control by the state that is not usually given to women. The state works to frame her professional behavior, experiences, and attitudes according to its androcentric priorities. (Dilley 58)

In looking at Dilley's claim, another of Sophie's contradictions appears. As an officer of the law, Sophie is separated from most women by her authority, an authority that has been granted and constructed by men. There is a code which she is expected to abide by, one that has been shaped by gendered priorities. Through her lies and deception, Sophie is working outside, and against, this patriarchal apparatus. However, although she is employing modes of agency, by framing them outside the social order she is aligned with the traditional models of injustice and immorality related to women in detective fiction.

At the crime scene, Sophie lies to Langdon telling him that there is a message for him from the US Embassy. She then gives him a slip of paper with a phone number and message code, which connects Langdon with Sophie's personal answering machine. There she has left a message instructing Langdon to tell Fache that there had been an accident with one of his friends back home, and to excuse himself to a nearby rest room. Although Fache and Langdon do not realize it at the time, she has already begun manipulating them and taking control of the situation. While Langdon is still on the phone, Sophie starts an argument with Fache and pretends to leave the Louvre. Instead of leaving, though, she meets up with Langdon in the rest room. Before she can explain her actions, Langdon observes her, and "was surprised to see that her strong air actually radiated from unexpectedly soft features. Only her gaze was sharp, and the juxtaposition conjured images of a multilayered Renoir portrait . . . veiled but distinct, with a boldness that somehow retained its shroud of mystery" (Brown 64). Here, any empowerment Sophie has gained is quickly underscored by Langdon's thoughts. Her "strong air" is tempered by her "soft" (i.e., womanly) features. Although some authority is given to *her* gaze, she is quickly identified with a portrait, something to be gazed upon, and appreciated, for its beauty. Further, her boldness remains shrouded by her feminine mystery.

Once Sophie's femininity is reestablished, she explains to Langdon that he is the prime suspect in Saunière's murder, and that Fache has planted a tracking device in Langdon's jacket so he can follow his every move in the Louvre. Sophie, believing in Langdon's innocence, flings the tracking device out the window onto a moving truck in order to throw Fache off-track and make him believe that Langdon has escaped. Dazed, "Langdon decided not to say another word all evening. Sophie Neveu was clearly a hell of a lot smarter than he was" (Brown 87).

Her intention is to take Langdon to the US Embassy for protection, but before they can leave, Langdon manages to figure out the code that Saunière has left on his body. Not only does this put the plot in motion, setting Langdon and Sophie off on a scavenger hunt of clues for the Holy Grail, but it also puts Langdon in the position of authority, showing that he is "clearly a hell of a lot smarter" than a female DCPJ cryptologist.

The second code that Langdon breaks before leaving the Louvre aligns Saunière with the Priory of Sion. As he explains to Sophie, "The Priory believes that Constantine and his male successors successfully converted the world from matriarchal paganism to patriarchal Christianity by waging a campaign of propaganda that demonized the sacred feminine, obliterating the goddess from modern religion forever" (Brown 124). This clue is important not only because it introduces the Priory, and Saunière's connection to the society into the story, but because it introduces the concept of the sacred feminine. Here the sacred feminine is not a symbol of virginal purity, but rather is aligned with Hieros Gamos, "the natural sexual union between man and women through which each became spiritually whole" (Brown 125). The sacred feminine signifies a dependency between the sexes based on equality and a balance of power.

As Sophie and Langdon continue to evade the police and follow the trail of clues, Langdon explains that the purpose of the Priory of Sion is to guard the secret of the Holy Grail. Further, "According to the Priory of Sion, the Holy Grail is not a cup at all. They claim the Grail legend–that of a *chalice*–is actually an ingeniously conceived allegory. That is, that the Grail story uses the *chalice* as a metaphor for something else, something far more powerful" (Brown 162). Before Langdon can explain to Sophie what this is, Sophie notices that the driver of the taxi they are in is attempting to radio authorities. Before he can make contact, "Sophie turned now and plunged her hand into the pocket of Langdon's tweed jacket. Before Langdon knew what had happened, she had yanked out the pistol, swung it around, and was pressing it to the back of the driver's head" (Brown 164). Here Sophie takes the active role in the scene, but it is tempered by the fact that she must gain her power from Langdon. She must reach into Langdon's pocket and remove his symbolic phallus, the gun, before she can gain control over the other man in the scene, the taxi driver. Still holding the gun, she orders Langdon to drive. "Langdon was not about to argue with a woman wielding a gun," so he begins to drive, despite the fact that he does not know how to operate a standard transmission (Brown 165). When it becomes apparent that he does not know what he is doing, Sophie, still in possession of the gun, takes over at the wheel, at ease with driving a stick. Although Sophie is clearly seen as the character in power, this power is only granted after she has taken possession of the weapon.

Without this phallus, Sophie's power is diminished. When Sophie and Langdon reach their destination, she instructs Langdon, "You'd better leave the gun here" (Brown 177). Their search has led them to a Swiss bank deposit box, and after retrieving the cryptex from the safety deposit, Sophie and Langdon escape with the help from the bank president, André Vernet. However it quickly becomes apparent he is not out to help the two, as he pulls a gun on them, forcing them from the armored truck in which they had escaped the bank.

Without her own gun, Sophie is helpless. Langdon, using both intelligence and physical strength, knocks Vernet down and the gun out of his hand. Sophie and Langdon quickly get back in the truck, this time with Langdon capably driving them to safety. Sitting in the passenger's seat, Sophie thinks, "Her grandfather's rationale for including him [Langdon] was now clear. Sophie was not equipped to understand her grandfather's intentions, and so he had assigned Robert Langdon as her guide. A tutor to oversee her education" (Brown 216). The balance of power has shifted from the earlier scene in the taxi. Robert is now in the driver's seat, both literally and figuratively, a position he will hold onto throughout the rest of the story. Sophie, "unequipped" to handle her grandfather's quest, is in many ways, just along for the ride.

Langdon takes Sophie to the home of Grail expert Sir Leigh Teabing. There Sophie, and readers, finally learn the "true" meaning of the Holy Grail. As it had already been established,

> The Grail is literally the ancient symbol for womanhood, and the *Holy* Grail represents the sacred feminine and the goddess, which of course has now been lost, virtually eliminated by the Church. The power of the female and her ability to produce life was once very sacred, but it posed a threat to the rise of the predominantly male Church, and so the sacred feminine was demonized and called unclean. (Brown 238)

Here it is re-established that the Grail is associated with the power of womanhood, but that the power is a threat to male dominance. As a result, the sacred feminine has been demonized. Although this statement is particularly referring to the sacred feminine, it is not a far stretch to see this as a representation of women historically. Seen as a threat to men, women have been rendered powerless and/or vilified. Stretching this analogy further, it also fits nicely with the aforementioned conventions of detective and mystery fiction, where women are demonized as seductresses or suspects, yet ultimately powerless to the control of men.

It is Teabing who finally reveals the truth behind the Holy Grail when he explains, "The legend of the Holy Grail is a legend about royal blood. When Grail legend speaks of 'the chalice that held the blood of Christ' . . . it speaks, in fact, of Mary Magdalene–the female womb that carried Jesus' royal bloodline" (Brown 249). He goes on to explain, "The Church, in order to defend itself against the Magdalene's power, perpetuated her image as a whore and buried evidence of Christ's marriage to her, thereby defusing any potential claims that Christ had a surviving bloodline and was a mortal prophet" (Brown 254). Here, the threat of women is directly linked with the power of their sexuality and ability to bear children. By characterizing Mary Magdalene as a whore, the text argues, history has been able to make her existence shameful and less of a threat.

Shortly after this explanation, the scene is interrupted by Saunière's murderer, Silas, who has come in search of the cryptex. After knocking Langdon unconscious, Silas aims his gun at Sophie. Brown writes, "Sophie Neveu, despite working in law enforcement, had never found herself at gunpoint until tonight" (276). In contrast to her earlier depictions, and despite the fact that she is a law enforcement agent, Sophie is helpless at this point. With Langdon temporarily out of commission, the only other character left to rescue her is Teabing. Here her helplessness is even more poignant, as she is aided by Teabing, a character already emasculated due to his physical handicap.

With the true nature of the Holy Grail finally revealed, the focus of the text shifts to what will happen once the protagonists find the Grail. Teabing strongly advocates sharing the Grail's secret, saying, "the Priory has not protected the truth all these years to have it gather dust until eternity. They have been waiting for the right moment in history to share their secret. A time when the world is ready to handle the truth" (Brown 295). Sophie, however, prefers "to trust that the Grail has found [her] for a reason, and when the time comes, [she] will know what to do" (Brown 295). Teabing thinks little of Sophie's opinion, finding her to be "light-years out of her league" (Brown 299). As soon as he reaches this conclusion, though, Sophie proves him to be wrong by breaking the next code. The back-and-forth opposition between these two characters is telling on a number of levels. Teabing, misogynistic towards Sophie, is the text's strongest proponent in revealing the Grail's secret. However, he wants the revelation to come from himself, a man. Further, although Teabing is initially aligned with the positive position of revealing the power of the sacred feminine, it is later discovered that he is the master mind behind the murder of Saunière and members of the Priory of Sion. His credibility, therefore, is diminished. Sophie, who as a woman should be for the exposing of the Holy Grail, is unsure.

A large part of her discomfort is due to her grandfather's involvement with the Priory of Sion. Sophie's estrangement from her grandfather stems from her witnessing his participation in Hieros Gamos, a ritualized sex orgy, some ten years earlier. As Langdon explains to Sophie,

> Historically, intercourse was the act through which male and female experienced God. The ancients believed that the male was spiritually incomplete until he had carnal knowledge of the sacred feminine. Physical union with the female remained the sole means through which man could become spiritually complete and ultimately achieve *gnosis*–knowledge of the divine. (Brown 308)

After accidentally seeing her grandfather engaged in Hieros Gamos, Sophie flees from his home, never to speak with him again. She does not even give him a chance to defend what was happening, despite his pleas over the years to explain. Here, Sophie is seen not only a prude, but also as unreasonable and irrational. Saunière was the only family she had, and she shut him out of her life without even allowing him to explain what she had witnessed.

Sophie continues to be haunted by this memory, reluctant to even discuss it with Langdon. When she does open up, she describes the scene: "Straddling her grandfather was a naked woman wearing a white mask, her luxuriant silver hair flowing out behind it. Her body was plump, far from perfect, and she was gyrating in rhythm to the chanting–making love to Sophie's grandfather" (Brown 311). In focusing on the female participant, "Here we find ourselves back in the traditional dynamics of the detective novel; female sexuality is a disruptive force that threatens the social order and must be punished" (Shuker-Haines 74). Not knowing the female partner, and thus unable to punish her, Sophie carries the punishment over to her grandfather. Further, Sophie's description of the scene adds to the objectification of women. Sophie sees this act as abhorrent, in part, because the woman does not fit the mold of feminine beauty. Her "silver hair" suggests age, and the body is "far from perfect" due to its weight. These attributes, coupled with the open sexuality of the act, disgust Sophie. Her rejection, along with her indecision regarding the grail, is a rejection of the sacred feminine.

Teabing, holding Sophie and Langdon at gunpoint, attempts to convince Sophie of her duty, saying, "Your grandfather's love for you prevented him from challenging the Church. His fear of reprisal against his only remaining family crippled him. He never had a chance to explain the truth because you rejected him, tying his hands, making him wait. Now you owe the world the truth" (Brown 409). Here, Sophie should be seen in a position of power. She has the ability to change the way the world has looked at history, and women, for the past two thousand years. While she grapples with her decision, however, the thoughts of the male characters severely undermine this power.

Assessing the situation with Teabing, Langdon thinks, "Despite the torrent of questions running through his mind, he knew only one thing mattered now–getting Sophie out of here alive . . . *I took her to Château Villette. I am responsible*" (Brown 409). With this sentence, Langdon has taken away whatever traces of empowerment Sophie had left. Not only is he not responsible for their situation, lest the reader forget that it was Sophie's initial plan that started the night's events, but nothing leading up to this point has suggested that Langdon is in any way capable of saving Sophie. However, as the plot reaches its climax, formula dictates that the characters must realign themselves in this way. For Sophie, this requirement means the woman that skillfully evaded Fache and planned the escape from the Louvre must be gone, leaving in her place, the conventional damsel in distress.

Teabing furthers the degradation of Sophie, saying, "'How was I to imagine the Grand Master would go to such ends to deceive me and bequeath the keystone to an estranged granddaughter?' Teabing looked at Sophie with disdain. 'Someone so unqualified to hold this knowledge that she required a symbologist baby-sitter?'" (Brown 411). Although this assessment initially seems to be unfair, it does bring up the question as to how a DCPJ cryptologist could be so inept at breaking codes, codes written by her own grandfather, nonetheless. Separating the two, "Teabing sensed he had successfully alienated the two companions from one another. Sophie Neveu remained defiant, but Langdon clearly saw the larger picture. He was trying to figure out the password. *He understands the importance of finding the Grail and releasing her from bondage*" (Brown 421). The "her" to which Teabing refers is Mary Magdalene, yet Langdon is more concerned with Sophie's well-being. In juxtaposing Sophie and Mary Magdalene this way, the characters are seen to be in opposition. However, because female equality has been in bondage for centuries, the character of Sophie must, therefore, be bound by generic conventions.

As the standoff between Teabing and Langdon reaches its conclusion, the positions of the characters are put in contrast. For Teabing, "Langdon's attempts to be gallant were more pathetic than anything. *On the verge of unveiling one of history's greatest secrets, and he troubles himself with a woman who has proven herself unworthy of the quest*" (Brown 422). Sophie, in a final attempt at control, declares, "'Robert, my grandfather would prefer his secret lost forever than see it in the hands of his murderer.' Sophie's eyes looked as if they would well with tears, but they did not. She stared directly back at Teabing. 'Shoot me if you have to. I am not leaving my grandfather's legacy in your hands'" (Brown 422). It would be foolish to suggest that as an individual life, Sophie is unimportant, but Teabing's thoughts do bring up an interesting dilemma: how does the importance of one life measure up against the history and oppression of millions? Sophie, in her attempts to be valiant, is not willing to sacrifice herself for the truth, but rather, for secrecy.

Given the Priory's true agenda in response to the Grail, Sophie's suggested sacrifice does not seem out of line. Like Sophie, the Priory is contradiction, a body that appears to be progressive, while ultimately perpetuating traditional gender stereotypes. On the one hand, "the Priory had always had female members. Four Grand Masters had been women. The *sénéchaux* were traditionally men–the guardians–and yet women held far more honored status within the Priory and could ascend to the highest post from virtually any rank" (Brown 444). In this way, the Priory embodies and promotes gender equality. However, despite the text's original assertion that the Priory was waiting for the right moment to reveal the Grail, Sophie's grandmother explains, "The Priory has always maintained that the Grail should *never* be unveiled" (Brown 444). After four hundred plus pages, not only is this a letdown to readers, but this statement completely undermines any positive claims the text may have attempted to make towards women's rights and equality.

When Langdon attempts to protest, Sophie's grandmother continues, "Her [Mary Magdalene's] story is being told in art, music, and books. More so every day. The pendulum is swinging. We are starting to sense the dangers of our history . . . and of our destructive paths. We are beginning to sense the need to restore the sacred feminine" (Brown 444). Perhaps "her" story is being told in art, music, and books, but are we really sensing the dangers of history? If *The Da Vinci Code* is the best example we have to answer that question, then the answer is a resounding "No."

The text goes on to say, "It is the mystery and wonderment that serve our souls, not the Grail itself. The beauty of the Grail lies in her ethereal nature . . . And for most, I suspect, the Holy Grail is simply a grand idea . . . a glorious unattainable treasure that somehow, even in today's world of chaos, inspires us" (Brown 444). After the text's pretense of empowerment, I find these lines extremely difficult to take. If we consider, as the text previously suggested, the Grail is a metaphor for female empowerment, then this passage can be interpreted to read, "It is the mystery and wonderment that serve our souls, not woman itself. The beauty of woman lies in her ethereal nature . . . And for most, I suspect, the sacred woman is simply a grand idea . . . a glorious unattainable treasure that somehow, even in today's world of chaos, inspires us." With this simple substitution, these lines reveal the misogynistic undertones that run throughout the text. It is the mystery and wonder surrounding women that serve a purpose to the text, not actual women. The beauty of women, their only asset, lies not in strength, but rather an ethereal (i.e., unearthly, fragile, or unsubstantial) nature. Therefore, anything sacred or powerful about women is a myth. In searching for the Holy Grail, the characters have been chasing a glorious, yet inevitably unattainable, treasure.

Looking specifically at how, like many forms of popular culture, *The Da Vinci Code* questions taboo sections of our society, in this case religion, sexuality, and gender roles, we see that the novel ultimately reinforces the very institutions it challenges. The text states, "the modern Bible was compiled and edited by men who possessed a political agenda–to promote the divinity of the man Jesus Christ and use His influence to solidify their own power base" (Brown 234). While I in no way desire to make comparisons between the Bible and *The Da Vinci Code*, this statement does help demonstrate the ways that popular texts reflect, and promote, political and hegemonic ideals. Further, "Popular fiction is not simply a product of the reader enjoying the novel, but also of its attraction to agents, editors, and publishers as a product that will generate revenue by attracting an audience with disposable income" (Dilley xvii). Conspiracies, religion, and sex not only make for a compelling story, but they sell well. *The Da Vinci Code* presents messy subjects in a neat and pretty package for an affluent and conservative audience.

Or, to place this idea in the context of genre,

> The conventions of the mystery novel comprise the system of codes that make meaning possible. The writer reaches out to the reader and society through the genre's codes. Readers and writers expand the conventions of genre by drawing attention to them and employing them in new situations. Genre fiction comments on society and its own conventions. Thus, it is both a reflection and a critique. (Dilley xvi)

As a mystery/detective novel, *The Da Vinci Code* works within the rules and conventions of genre fiction. Using religion and gender to develop inventions, *The Da Vinci Code* draws upon taboo issues in culture, commenting, as Dilley states, "on society and its own conventions." Although *The Da Vinci Code* may be attempting to critique society's position on both religion and women, ultimately it confirms the authority of the very institutions it questions. Specifically in respect to women, "The message of the detective novel is that any changes in social organization that arise from women's active participation in public life can be dismissed by the reader as short-lived and inconsequential" (Dilley 58). The text goes to extremes getting this point across by systematically stripping Sophie of power and control, and ultimately denouncing the idea of the sacred feminine.

If, "the 'feminisation' of certain popular texts provides an opportunity to analyze the way they provide an understanding of the marginalization of women and how that marginalization may be resisted by still locating women within acceptably feminine parameters," *The Da Vinci Code* suggests that marginalization cannot be avoided (Devas 251). Detective fiction has evolved over the last couple of decades to allow women to have positions of authority, removing them from what Devas terms "acceptably feminine parameters." The Miss Marples and Jessica Fletchers may have been pushed aside to make room for their more powerful and authoritative sisters, but at what cost? As Devas suggested, under their blatant sexist constraints, traditional mystery and detective texts at least left some room for women's resistance against marginalization. Conversely, under the guise of inoculation, texts such as *The Da Vinci Code* appear to give audiences legitimate models of female agency, but as a closer examination reveals, these women come in a much tighter overall package of patriarchy.

At the end of *The Da Vinci Code*, Langdon figures out the final clue to where the Holy Grail lies. Upon this realization, the final lines of the text are,

"For a moment, he thought he heard a woman's voice . . . the wisdom of the ages . . . whispering up from the chasms of the earth" (Brown 454). If academics and audiences are unwilling to look at popular texts with a critical eye, unwilling to engage in struggles at the site of where they are currently happening, then texts such as *The Da Vinci Code* will function little more than to perpetuate dominant ideology. Gender equality exists as a concept; however, academics and audiences need to start making some noise for it to register as more than a whisper.

Works Cited

Brown, Dan. *The Da Vinci Code*. New York: Random House, 2003.

Devas, Angela. "Murder, Mass Culture, and the Feminine: A View From the 4.50 From Paddington." *Feminist Media Studies* 2.2 (2002): 251-265.

Dilley, Kimberly J. *Busybodies, Meddlers, and Snoops: The Female Hero in Contemporary Women's Mysteries*. Connecticut: Greenwood Press, 1998.

Mizejewski, Linda. *Hardboiled and High Heeled: The Woman Detective in Popular Culture.* New York: Routledge, 2004.

Shuker-Haines, Timothy, and Martha M. Umphrey. "Gender (De)Mystified: Resistance and Recuperation in Hard-Boiled Female Detective Fiction." *The Detective in American Fiction, Film, and Television.* Ed. Jerome H. Delamater and Ruth Prigozy. Connecticut: Greenwood Press, 1998. 71-84.

CONTRIBUTORS

Jenn Brandt is a master's student and graduate teaching assistant in the department of Popular Culture at Bowling Green State University. Her work focuses primarily on gender studies, television, and popular literature.

Harry Brown is Assistant Professor of English at DePauw University. He is the author of *Injun Joe's Ghost: The Indian Mixed-Blood in American Writing* (U of Missouri P, 2004).

Robert A. Davis is Head of the Department of Religious Education at the University of Glasgow He has edited and introduced the books *Robert Graves and Raphael Patai, The Hebrew Myths* (Manchester: Carcanet, 2005) and *Robert Graves, King Jesus and My Head! My Head!* (Manchester: Carcanet, 2006) and contributed the following articles: "Education, Utopia and the Limits of Enlightenment," in M. Peters and J. Freeman-moir, *Edutopias: New Utopian Thinking in Education* (Rotterdam: Sense Publishers, 2006); "Seeing Everything at Once: Myth, Freedom and Determinism in Alan Garner's The Owl Service and Red Shift," in Justyna Descz-Tryhubczak and Marek Oziewicz (Eds), *Towards or Back to Human Values? Spiritual Dimensions of Contemporary Fantasy* (Newcastle: Cambridge Scholars Press, 2006); "The Black Goddess," in I. Firla and G. Lindop (Eds), *Graves and the Goddess: Essays on Robert Graves's The White Goddess* (London: Associated University Presses, 2003).

Arlette Poland is a PhD student in Women's Studies in Religion at Claremont Graduate University and she teaches in the Religion Department at the University of Redlands, California. She has written "God's Power is Not Persuasive, Anymore" Creative Transformation (Center for Process and Faith: Winter 2006) and "Power Thinking: An Introduction to Your Power" (Center for Process and Faith: 2003) and was a contributing writer of "Process Perspectives" (Center for Process & Faith: Spring 2002 and Spring 2004).

Rosa Maria Stoops is Assistant Professor of Spanish in the English and Foreign Languages Department at the University of Montevallo. She is the author of "The Interior Alchemy: The Transformation of the Individual Through Literature" in *Proceedings of the Hermes and Aphrodite Colloquium in Contemporary Literature and Culture*, (Tuscaloosa, AL: University of Alabama Press, 2005).

Deanna A. Thompson is Chair and Associate Professor of Religion at Hamline University. She is the author of *Crossing the Divide: Luther, Feminism, and the Cross* (Fortress Press, 2004) and "Becoming a Feminist Theologian of the Cross," in *Cross Examinations: Reflections on the Meaning of the Cross Today* (Fortress, 2006).

Rachel Wagner is Assistant Professor of Religion at Ithaca College. She has co-authored with Dr. Frances Flannery-Dailey "Wake Up! Gnosticism and Buddhism in *The Matrix*" in the *Journal of Religion and Film* (Vol. 5, No. 2, October 2002; "Stopping Bullets: Constructions of Bliss and Problems of Violence," in *Jacking-in to The Matrix* (Continuum Press, 2004); and "Ultimate Reality: Gnostic and Buddhist Constructions of Bliss" in *Free Your Mind,* an anthology of works on philosophy and religion forthcoming from Oxford Press.

INDEX